The Plutarch Project

Volume Nine

Alcibiades, Coriolanus, and Cato the Younger

by

Anne E. White

The Plutarch Project Volume Nine:

Cover photograph: Anne White. Cover design: Bryan White

ISBN: 978-1-7772522-4-3

CONTENTS

Introduction

These notes, and the accompanying text, are prepared for the use of individual students and small groups following a twelve-week term. The text is a free mixture of Thomas North's 1579 translation of Plutarch's *Lives of the Noble Greeks and Romans* and John Dryden's 1683 translation. (North for character, Dryden for clarity.)

Please note that some omissions have **not** been noted. Those using audio versions or other translations may want to preview those versions for suitability.

Using the Lesson Material

Each study contains explanatory material before the first lesson. A little at the beginning may be useful to stir interest in the study, but it is not meant to be given all in one dose!

Some lessons are divided into two or three sections. These can be read all at once or used throughout the week.

I encourage you to make the lessons your own. Use the questions that are the most meaningful to you. Remember that Charlotte Mason was satisfied with "Proper names are written on the blackboard, and then the children narrate what they have listened to."

Examination Questions

The three studies include suggestions for end-of-term examinations. The questions for *Alcibiades* and *Coriolanus* were drawn from original P.N.E.U. programmes, and those for *Cato the Younger* were written for this volume.

How did Plutarch write a story?

One of the difficulties in beginning to read Plutarch, especially for young readers, is that it's not immediately clear a) what kind of a story this is, and b) who the characters are in the story. Not all the people named are actually part of the main character's life; some of them are historians, poets or others who wrote about him later on.

Imagine that you get an assignment to write the story of someone's life. You're allowed to use any books or other documents you can find on that person; but since he or she lived a hundred or more years ago, there are no eyewitnesses who can clear up questions or contradictions. You just have to do the best you can with what's available. Plutarch used bits of plays and poems, historical accounts, sometimes even graffiti or jokes, to construct a whole picture of whoever he was writing about. And he was usually careful to give credit to his sources. He might say, "So and so the historian tells this anecdote about Alcibiades' childhood," and then go on for a few paragraphs telling the story. So there is a hint for making sense of Plutarch's narrative: watch for his transitions and the places where he begins telling what someone else said. Sometimes Plutarch does this in such a rapid-fire style that it's hard to keep up with him; but, fast or slow, it's the same thing: using bits and pieces, making connections, and trying to pull the whole thing together with his unique moral emphasis.

One more note: Plutarch often says, "It is said," and then goes on to tell what might have happened; but then he undercuts himself and says something like, "But the best sources disagree with that story." You might then wonder why he troubled himself to include something of doubtful accuracy; but it seems he wants to include all the possibilities.

Alcibiades

(c. 450-404 B.C.)

Why study Alcibiades?

Even scholars who have studied Alcibiades for years are still trying to decide if his accomplishments outweigh his mistakes and faults.For Plutarch, there are two "telling details" about Alcibiades: the sight of him flouncing along the street in a purple robe; and the extra-soft bed that he had fitted out on his warship. Neither of these examples, in Plutarch's opinion, showed the right kind of dignity, resolve or courage for a virtuous leader. In the case of Alcibiades, his double-dealing and lack of personal restraint (including his involvement with the wife of a Spartan king) eventually led to a horrible death.

So why study Alcibiades, particularly in our context of character and citizenship studies? Do we read it only as a negative example of what not to do? Do we admire his intelligence, if not his ethics?

I would like to suggest at least two reasons. First, when we look at Alcibiades himself, we learn something about the qualities necessary for leadership, and see how those qualities were or weren't apparent in his life. What mistakes did he make? How did he become powerful, and how did he abuse that power?

Second, we can consider the role that citizens play in civil affairs. How can we choose our leaders carefully? What basis do we have for following someone or turning against him? How do we react if we think our leaders have done wrong? There is much to consider here about crowd behaviour and the effects of propaganda.

> **A Dividing Line.**—Both Shakespeare and Scott use, as it were, a dividing line, putting on the one side the wilful, wayward, the weak and the strong; and on the other, persons who will...To make even a suggestive list would be to range over all history and literature. Let me say again, however, that here is a line of study which should make our reading profitable, as making us intimate with persons, and the more able for life. (Charlotte Mason, *Ourselves*)

Alcibiades' World

The city-state of Athens had a system of **democratic** government (government "by the people") which was unusual at that time. Its people believed that everyone could and should contribute to the life of the city: because the city wasn't where they lived, *they* were the city. Athens was ruled by an assembly of male citizens, with the intention that all their voices should be heard equally.

The goddess **Athena** (also called **Pallas Athena**) for whom Athens was named, wore armour and was called the goddess of victory, but she was also in charge of wisdom and the arts. There is a legend that when Athena's temple was destroyed in the Persian Wars, a tiny olive shoot (the olive was her special tree) sprouted on the temple site as a sign of hope and rebirth. The Athenians put their faith in that sign, and their efforts into building something both beautiful and strong in her honour.

But Athens was, in fact, nearing the end of its power as a city/state. After the Peloponnesian War (fought mainly between Athens and Sparta, but also involving the Persians), Athenian power and culture were never the same again. (Alcibiades died during the last year of that war.)

The Geography: Map Work

Greece is divided almost in two by the **Isthmus of Corinth**. The southern section, containing **Sparta** or **Lacedaemonia**, is called the **Peloponnesus**. Athens did not get along very well with the cities in the Peloponnesus, particularly Sparta and **Corinth**.

Attica was the name for the region of Greece which included the city-state of **Athens**. The word **Attic** or **Attican** is sometimes used to describe aspects of Athenian life and culture, such as the "Attic dialect." Attica was bordered by the **Aegean Sea** to the east, **Boeotia** to the north, and **Megara** to the west. You will find it useful to have maps not only of Greece in the fifth century B.C., but also of the **Persian Empire**, as much of the action in this story takes place in regions such as **Asia Minor**.

The Timeline: Wars and More Wars

(Those who have already done the *Life of Pericles* will have already done the following exercise, and if they still have that timeline, it can be extended for Alcibiades.)

Make a timeline or chart showing the years 500-400 B.C. Mark (circle or shade) the fifty years between 480-430 B.C. This is the period considered the "Golden Age" of Athens. Mark the birth of Alcibiades in approximately 450, and his death in 404. You might also note two major events of his life: his exile from Athens beginning in 415, and his return sometime between 410 and 407.

With one colour, shade in or circle the years 499-449, the span of the Greco-Persian Wars. With a second colour, mark the years 460-445, the First Peloponnesian War. The proposed "Thirty Years' Peace" between Athens and Sparta began in 446/445, when Alcibiades was a small child. With a third colour, mark 431-404, the Second Peloponnesian War (also called just the Peloponnesian War), which began as Alcibiades was entering adulthood. Note how few years of that century there were in which Athens was not involved in conflict.

Top Vocabulary Terms in the *Life of Alcibiades*

1. **barbarians, barbarous:** foreign, and particularly Persian. This term did not carry the weight we give to it now (it was a bit negative, but not insulting).
2. **commonwealth:** a city or state and its colonies or dependencies; in this case, Athens and its satellite cities
3. **credit:** believe
4. **divers:** sometimes means "different," but often means "several"
5. **eloquence:** the art of fluent or persuasive speaking or writing
6. **faction:** small group within a larger one, often relating to a dispute or position on an issue
7. **galley:** a ship with sails and banks of oars, used for trade and war (also for piracy)
8. **satrap:** in the Persian empire, the governor of a province
9. **stay:** stop or delay
10. **voices:** votes, except in reference to Thrasybulus #1 (**Lesson Eight**), the man with the biggest and loudest voice in Athens

Lesson One

Introduction

Alcibiades was born in the Greek city-state of Athens, at a time when a long war with the still-mighty Persian empire was ending, and when the mood of the city was triumphant and optimistic. He grew up under the guardianship of Pericles, a famous general who was then busy with great building projects on the Acropolis.

And Alcibiades himself, from the very beginning, stood out from the crowd.

Vocabulary

Of all fair things...: Alcibiades was as attractive in maturity as he had been in his youth

happy constitution: good health

the many and wonderful vicissitudes...: the amazing amount of ups and downs he survived

hardly: roughly

knave: rascal

flute: or pipe; probably the ancient wind instrument called the *aulos*

sordid: sleazy, low-class

articulation: formation of sounds

stripped the flute-player of his skin: this refers to the story of Apollo and the satyr Marsyas, who, some believe, invented the *aulos* (or picked it up after **Athena** discarded it, see below).

incontinently: quickly, without restraint

honest and liberal exercises: respectable things to do

vile: ugly, disgusting

People

Pericles: Athenian statesman and general

Socrates: The philosopher Socrates was about twenty years older than Alcibiades, but outlived him by five years.

Euripides: Athenian writer of tragedies

Pallas: or **Athena**; the patron goddess of Athens. She seems to have agreed with Alcibiades about playing the flute: legend says that she threw the aulos away because it made her cheeks puff out.

Apollo: a major Greek god

Historic Occasions

Please read the introductory note on timelines for this study.

495 B.C.: Birth of Pericles

c. 470 B.C.: Births of Socrates and Nicias

451-449/448 B.C.: Official end of the Greco-Persian Wars

c. 450 B.C.: Birth of Alcibiades

447 B.C.: Death of Alcibiades' father Cleinias at the Battle of Coronea

447 B.C.: Construction begun on the Parthenon

446/445 B.C.: Thirty Years' Peace declared between Athens and Sparta

438 B.C.: Work completed on the Parthenon

On the Map

See the introductory notes for help with the first lesson.

Artemisium: or Artemision; a cape (point of land) in northern Euboea; the site of a major battle during the Persian Wars

Coronea: a town in **Boeotia**

Boeotia: a region of Central Greece, which sided with Sparta during the Peloponnesian War

Thebes (children of the Thebans): The city of Thebes in Boeotia was known as a center of aulos-playing. Alcibiades' objection to playing the flute may have been cultural rather than just personal.

Reading

Part One

Alcibiades, as it is supposed, was anciently descended of Eurysaces, the son of Ajax, by his father's side; and by his mother's side, from Alcmaeon. Dinomache, his mother, was the daughter of Megacles. His father, Cleinias, having armed and set forth a galley at his own costs and charges, did win great honour in the battle by sea that was fought at **Artemisium**; and he was slain afterwards in another battle fought at **Coronea**, against the **Boeotians**.

Pericles and Ariphron, the sons of Xanthippus and closely related to him, became the guardians of Alcibiades.

[Plutarch points out that because of Alcibiades' fame via his friendship with ***Socrates,*** *we know not only the name of his mother but even that of his Lacedaemonian nursemaid, Amycla, and his teacher-attendant, Zopyrus.]*

Now for Alcibiades' beauty, it makes no matter if we speak not of it; only that it bloomed with him in all the ages of his life, in his infancy, in his youth, and in his manhood; and, in the peculiar character becoming to each of these periods, gave him, in every one of them, a grace and a charm. What **Euripides** says, that—

> **Of all fair things the autumn, too, is fair**,

is by no means universally true. But it happened so with Alcibiades, amongst few others, by reason of his **happy constitution** and natural vigour of body. It is said that his lisping, when he spoke, became him well, and gave a grace and persuasiveness to his rapid speech.

[omission for length]

Part Two

His conduct displayed many great inconsistencies and variations, not unnaturally, in accordance with **the many and wonderful vicissitudes of his fortunes**; but among the many strong passions of his real character, the one most prevailing of all was his ambition and desire of superiority: as appeareth by certain of his deeds, and notable sayings in his youth. One day wrestling with a companion of his, that handled him **hardly**, and thereby was likely to have given him the fall: he got his fellow's arm in his mouth, and bit so hard as he would have bitten it off. The other, feeling him bite so hard, let go his hold straight, and said unto him: "Alcibiades, thou bitest like a woman!" "No, that I do not," quoth he, "but like a lion."

Another time being but a little boy, he played at dice in the midst of the street with his companions; and when his turn came about to throw, there came a cart laden, by chance, that way. Alcibiades prayed the carter to stay a while, until he had played out his game, because the dice were set right in the highway where the cart should pass over. The carter was a stubborn **knave**, and would not stay for any request the boy could make, but drove his horse on still, insomuch as other boys gave back to let him go on: but Alcibiades fell flat to the ground before the cart, and bade the carter drive over if he dared. This so startled the man that he put back his horses; while all that saw it were terrified, and, crying out, they ran to assist Alcibiades.

Afterwards when he was put to school to learn, he was very obedient to all his masters that taught him anything, but refused to learn upon the **flute**, as a **sordid** thing, and not becoming a free citizen; saying that to play on the lute or the harp does not in any way disfigure a man's body or face, but one is hardly to be known by the most intimate friends when playing on the flute. Besides, one who plays on the harp may speak or sing at the same time; but the use of the flute stops the mouth, intercepts the voice, and prevents all **articulation**.

"Therefore," said he, "let the **children of the Thebans** play on the flute, that cannot tell how to speak: as for us Athenians, we have (as our forefathers tell us) for protectors and patrons of our country, the goddess **Pallas**, and the god **Apollo**: of the which the one in old time (as it is said) broke the flute, and the other **stripped the flute-player of his skin**." Thus Alcibiades alleging these reasons, partly in sport, and partly in good earnest, did not only himself refuse to learn to play on the flute, but he turned his companions' minds also quite from it. For these words of Alcibiades ran from boy to boy **incontinently**: that Alcibiades had reason to despise playing of the flute, and that he mocked all those that learned to play of it. So afterwards, it fell out at Athens, that teaching to play of the flute was put out of the number of **honest and liberal exercises**; and the flute itself was thought a **vile** instrument, and of no reputation.

[omission for content]

Narration and Discussion

Consider the various anecdotes about Alcibiades' childhood: the biting story, the dice story, the story about refusing to play the flute because it made him look silly. What do all of these show you so far about his character? What opinion did Alcibiades have of himself?

Creative narration: Write or act out a scene using one of the following imaginary characters: an Athenian dealer in musical instruments; the delivery driver when he returned to his shop; a "school nurse" who deals with frequent Alcibiades-related incidents.

Lesson Two

Introduction

As a young man, Alcibiades was in danger of being completely ruined by those who flattered his good looks and who wanted to make use of his political ambition. However, he did have one true friend who seemed to push him towards better things.

Vocabulary

station: status, position

interpose: intervene; put oneself between two things

Fortune: Plutarch refers to Fortune as a female deity

unnerve: To "unnerve" someone usually means to scare them or make them lose confidence; here it means to make someone unsteady, to deprive them of strength (particularly moral strength).

happiness of his genius: positive (or fortunate) aspect of his character. "Genius" in the ancient world also referred to a person's attendant spirit, something that protected or assisted them. In this case we could say "It was his good Fortune…"

discerned: picked out

dropped like the craven cock...: lost his arrogance, became humble

He esteemed these endeavours of Socrates...: He valued Socrates' wisdom as a godsend to young men in general, and to himself particularly

made their addresses, courted him: flattered him, sought his company

stater: a Greek coin

where the farms and lands...: an event where farmland was leased (rented) for the year to the highest bidders

hire: rent

talent: a unit of money. In Ancient Greece, a talent was about 57 pounds (26 kg) of silver.

surety: one who promises to be responsible for another's debt

relinquish: give up

relieved his necessity: took care of his need. (The phrase is used in Philippians 4:16.)

betimes: when he was not yet ready

blemish and deface: Dryden says "obscure"; wipe from memory

People

Anteros: In Greek mythology, Anteros was the god of returned love, and the punisher of those who scorned it

Reading

Part One

Now straight there were many great and rich men that made much of Alcibiades, and were glad to get his goodwill. But the affection which Socrates entertained for him is a great evidence of the natural noble qualities and good disposition of the boy; which Socrates, indeed, detected both in and under his personal beauty; and, hearing that his wealth and **station**, and the great number both of strangers and Athenians who flattered and caressed him, might at last corrupt him, resolved, if possible, to **interpose**, and preserve so hopeful a plant from perishing in the flower, before its fruit came to perfection.

For never did **Fortune** surround and enclose a man with so many of those things which we vulgarly call "goods," or so protect him from every weapon of philosophy, and fence him from every access of free and searching words, as she did Alcibiades; who, from the beginning, was shut up as it were in the company of those who feasted him with all pleasures, such as might well **unnerve** him, and indispose him to listen to any real advisor or instructor. Yet such was the **happiness of his genius** that he **discerned** Socrates from the rest, and went to him, refusing the company of all his rich friends and their flatteries, and fell in a kind of familiar friendship with Socrates. And Alcibiades, finding himself with one who sought to lay open to him the deficiencies of his mind, and repress his vain and foolish arrogance—

Dropped like the craven cock his conquered wing.

He esteemed these endeavours of Socrates most truly a means which the gods made use of for the care and preservation of youth; and began to think meanly of himself and to admire him; to be pleased with his kindness, and to stand in awe of his virtue; and unawares to himself, there became formed in his mind that reflex image and reciprocation of Love, or **Anteros**, that Plato talks of. It was a matter of general wonder, when people saw him joining Socrates in his meals and his exercises, living with him in the same tent, whilst he was reserved and rough to all others who **made their addresses** to him.

[omission for length and content]

Part Two

He behaved with insolence to all those who **courted him**, except only one stranger, who, as the story is told, having but a small estate, sold it all for about a hundred **staters**, which he presented to Alcibiades, and besought him to accept. Alcibiades, smiling and well pleased at the thing, invited him to supper. When supper was done, he gave him his money again, and commanded him not to fail the next morning to meet him **where the farms and lands of the city are wont to be let out to those that bid most**, and charged him he should outbid all. The poor man would fain have excused himself, saying that the farms were too great for him to **hire**: but Alcibiades threatened to whip him if he would not do it. For besides the desire he had to pleasure him, he bore a private grudge against the ordinary farmers of the city.

The next morning the stranger was ready in the marketplace, where they did cry out the letting of their farms; and he raised one to a **talent** more than all others did offer. The other farmers were as mad with him as they could be, so that they all did call upon him to name his **sureties**, supposing he could have found none. The stranger was marvellous blank thereat, and began to shrink back.

Then Alcibiades cried out aloud to the officers that sat there to take the best offers: "I will be his surety. Put me in the book, for he is a friend of mine." The farmers, hearing him say so, were at their wits' end and knew not what to do. For their way was, with the profits of the second year, to pay the rent for the year preceding; so that, not seeing any other way to extricate themselves out of the difficulty, they began to entreat the stranger, and offered him a sum of money to leave the bargain. Alcibiades would not allow him to accept of less than a talent; but when that was paid down, he commanded him to **relinquish** the bargain, having by this device **relieved his necessity**.

Part Three

Though Socrates had many and powerful rivals, yet the natural good qualities of Alcibiades gave his affection the mastery. His words overcame him so much, as to draw tears from his eyes, and to disturb his very soul. Yet sometimes he would abandon himself to flatterers, when they proposed to him varieties of pleasure, and would desert Socrates; who, then, would pursue him as if he had been a fugitive slave *[omission for content]*.

Those who endeavoured to corrupt Alcibiades took advantage chiefly of his vanity and ambition, and did put him in the head to thrust himself into great matters **betimes**; making him believe that if he did but once begin to show himself to deal in matters of state, he would not only **blemish and deface** all other governors, but far excel Pericles in authority and power among the Greeks. For like as iron by fire is made soft, to be wrought into any form, and by cold also doth shut and harden in again: so, as often as Socrates observed Alcibiades to be puffed up with vanity and opinion of himself, he reduced and corrected him by his addresses, and made him humble and modest, by showing him in how many things he was deficient, and how very far from perfection in virtue.

Narration and Discussion

Someone may be "corrupt," meaning that they are dishonest or immoral; but someone may also be "corrupted" by others; that is, causing them to lose their potential good character. How did those who sought to corrupt Alcibiades make use of his vanity and ambition?

For older students: North's translation of Part Three begins in this way: "Now Socrates' love which he bore him, though it had many mighty and great adversaries, yet it did stay much Alcibiades, sometime by his gentle nature, sometime by his grave counsel and advice: so as the reason thereof took deep root in him, and did so pierce his heart, that many times the tears ran down his cheeks." Write an imagined scene to illustrate this description.

Lesson Three

Introduction

This lesson continues the series of anecdotes and incidents which introduce us to Alcibiades. We begin to see how, in spite of (or possibly because of) his eccentricities, he achieved the high level of public respect that led to his being made commander of the Athenian navy.

Vocabulary

Homer's books: The *Iliad* and the *Odyssey*

box: swat, punch

corrected: edited

how he might avoid giving up his accounts at all: This translation misses the humour intended by Alcibiades' remark. Pericles was trying to figure out how to show his accounts; Alcibiades said that he should spend the time working out how *not* to show his accounts.

skirmish: a battle, usually unplanned

signal: significant

mina: a unit of money equaling originally 70 and later 100 **drachmae**

largess: gift, donation

transported: excited and happy

quail: It seems strange that anyone would be carrying a quail under their robe (or cloak), but apparently the Greeks played a gambling game with them called *ortygokopia* (don't look it up, it involves hitting birds); and Alcibiades was such a fan that he carried one around with him in case he had the opportunity for a game.

contending which should gratify him best: each trying to please him the most

censure: criticism, scolding

People

Antiochus: a naval commander (we will hear more about him later)

Demosthenes: Athenian statesman who lived in the century before Alcibiades, famed for his skill in oration

Theophrastus: a scholar who lived after Alcibiades; known as the "Father of Botany"

Phaeax: a rival orator

Nicias: Athenian politician and general; the main political rival of Alcibiades; subject of Plutarch's *Nicias*

Historic Occasions

434/432 B.C.: Battle of Potidaea (precursor to the Peloponnesian War)

431 B.C.: Archidamus of Sparta invaded Attica; beginning of the Second Peloponnesian War

430 B.C.: Plague of Athens, described in Plutarch's *Life of Pericles*

429 B.C.: Death of Pericles

424 B.C.: Battle of Delium, between the Athenians and the Boeotians

c. 422 B.C.: Alcibiades entered politics (in his late twenties)

On the Map

Ephesus (Ephesians): a city on the coast of Ionia (in present-day Turkey)

Chios: an island in the northern Aegean Sea

Lesbos: an island in the northeastern Aegean Sea

Argos (Argives): a city in Argolis, in the Peloponnese; known for being one of the oldest continuously inhabited cities in the world

Reading

Part One

When he was past his childhood, he went once into a grammar school, and asked the schoolmaster for one of **Homer's books**. The schoolmaster answered him that he had none of them: Alcibiades swung up with his fist, and gave him a good **box** on the ear, and went his way. Another grammarian told him on a time he had Homer which he had "**corrected**." Alcibiades replied, "Why, what meanest thou to stand teaching little children the alphabet, when thou art able to correct Homer, and to teach young men, not boys?"

Another time he came and knocked at Pericles' gate, desirous to speak with him: answer was made him that Pericles was not at leisure now, for that he was busily occupied by himself, thinking on his reckonings he had to make with the Athenians. Alcibiades, as he went away, said, "It were better for him to consider **how he might avoid giving up his accounts at all**."

Part Two

When he was very young, he was a soldier in the expedition against **Potidaea**, where Socrates lodged in the same tent with him, and stood next to him in battle. Once there happened a sharp **skirmish**, in which they both behaved with **signal** bravery; but Alcibiades receiving a wound, Socrates threw himself before him to defend him, and beyond any question saved him and his arms from the enemy; and so in all justice might have challenged the prize of valour.

So the honour of this fight out of doubt, in equity and reason, was due unto Socrates: but yet the captains would fain have judged it on Alcibiades' side, because he was of a noble house. But Socrates, because he would increase his (Alcibiades') desire of honour, and would prick him forward to honest and commendable things, was the very first that witnessed Alcibiades had deserved it: and therefore prayed the captains to judge him the crown and complete armour.

Afterwards, in the **Battle of Delium**, the Athenians having received the overthrow, Socrates retreated with a few others afoot. Alcibiades, being a-horseback, and overtaking him, would not go from him, but kept him company, and brought him safe off, though the enemy pressed hard upon them, and cut off many. But this happened sometime after.

Part Three

[omission for content: the troubled relationship between Alcibiades and his wife Hipparete]

Alcibiades had a dog which cost him seventy **minas**, and it was a very large one, and very handsome. His tail, which was his principal ornament, he caused to be cut off; and his acquaintances exclaiming at him for it, and telling him that all Athens was sorry for the dog, and crying out upon him for this action, he laughed, and said, "Just what I wanted has happened then. I wished the Athenians to talk about this, that they might not say something worse of me."

The first time that Alcibiades spoke openly in the commonwealth, and began to deal in matters, was upon occasion of a **largess** of money which he made to the people. This (gift) was not done by design, but as he passed along he heard a shout, and inquiring the cause, they told him it was about money certain men had given to the people. Then Alcibiades went to them, and gave them money out of his own purse. The multitude thereupon applauding him, and shouting, he was so **transported** at it, that he forgot a **quail** which he had under his robe. The bird, being frighted with the noise, flew off, upon which the people made louder acclamations than before, and many of them started up to pursue the bird; but one **Antiochus**, a pilot, caught it and restored it to him, for which he was ever after a favourite with Alcibiades.

Part Four

He had great advantages for entering public life: his noble birth, his riches, the personal courage he had shown in divers battles, and the multitude of his friends and dependents, threw open, so to say, folding-doors for his admittance. Yet the only way he desired to win the favour of the common people was by the grace of his eloquence. That he was a master in the art of speaking, the comic poets bear him witness; and **Demosthenes**, the most eloquent of public speakers, in his oration against Midias, allows that Alcibiades, among other perfections, was a most accomplished orator. If, however, we give credit to **Theophrastus**, who of all philosophers was the most curious inquirer, and the greatest lover of history, we are to understand that Alcibiades had the highest capacity for inventing, for discerning what was the right thing to be said for any purpose, and on any occasion; but aiming not only at saying what was required, but also at saying it well; in respect, that is, of words and phrases; when these did not readily occur, he would often pause in the middle of his discourse for want of the apt word, and would be silent and stop till he could recollect himself, and had considered what to say.

[omission for length]

Howbeit the good affection divers cities did bear him, **contending which should gratify him best**, did much increase his fame and honour. For the **Ephesians** did set up a tent for him, very sumptuously and richly furnished. The city of **Chios** furnished him with provender for his horses, and with great numbers of beasts for sacrifice; and those of **Lesbos** sent him wine and other provisions for the many great entertainments which he made.

Yet in the midst of all this he escaped not without **censure**, occasioned either by the ill-nature of his enemies or by his own misconduct. For it is said that one Diomedes, an Athenian, a worthy man and a friend to Alcibiades, passionately desiring to obtain the victory at the Olympic games, and having heard much of a chariot which belonged to the state at **Argos**, where he knew that Alcibiades had great power and many friends, prevailed with him to undertake to buy the chariot. Alcibiades did indeed buy it, but then claimed it for his own, leaving Diomedes to rage at him, and to call upon the gods and men to bear witness to the injustice.

[omission for length]

As soon as Alcibiades began to intermeddle in the government, which was when he was very young, he quickly lessened the credit of all who aspired to the confidence of the people, except **Phaeax** the son of Erasistratus, and **Nicias** the son of Niceratus, who alone could contest it with him. Of these two, Nicias was a man grown, and was esteemed their first general. Phaeax was but a rising statesman like Alcibiades; he was descended from noble ancestors, but was his inferior, as in many other things, so, principally, in eloquence. He could more properly talk and discourse among his friends privately than he had any good grace to open a matter openly before the people. For he had, as Eupolis sayeth:

> Words enough, but no eloquence.

There is a certain oration extant in writing, against Alcibiades, by Phaeax: in which, amongst other things, it is said that Alcibiades made daily use at his table of many gold and silver vessels, which belonged to the commonwealth, as if they had been his own.

Narration and Discussion

Why did Socrates insist that Alcibiades receive the medal at Potidaea? Do you think Alcibiades learned anything from his example?

Alcibiades wanted to be known for his eloquence. Why was this so important to him? Was he successful?

Describe Alcibiades' attitude towards money and material things.

For older students: Charlotte Mason described the difference between those who live according to Will (those who recognize the need to act, and who live with a purpose or object outside of themselves), and those who live Willfully (trapped by their own desires). Those acting with Will may be immoral, but they are still distinguished from those who simply want whatever catches their attention today.

> "[A wilful person] is steady to only one thing, he must always have his own way; but his way is a will-o'-the-wisp which leads him in many directions...He is a wilful man, without power or desire to control the lead of his nature..." (*Ourselves Book II*, p. 130)

Does Alcibiades, as you have seen him so far, fit into one or the other of those groups? Give examples. If you need comparisons, there is a list on page 134 of *Ourselves Book II*, which puts Faust and Lady Macbeth under "Willful," and Sir Thomas More, and Mary Queen of Scots under "Will."

You may want to revisit this later in the study.

Lesson Four

Introduction

Plutarch begins this section with a rare example of Alcibiades and Nicias working together: in this case, to make sure that a third (and very troublesome) person was ostracized, instead of either of them.

This incident actually happened sometime later, just before the **Sicilian Expedition**; but it does introduce us to the growing rivalry that was growing between the two leaders.

Vocabulary

magistrate: local ruler, especially one who judges court cases

when peace was concluded: This was not the end of the war, but only the first half of it, agreed upon by the "Peace of Nicias." The terms of the treaty were broken almost from the start, and it was abandoned in 414 B.C. when the fighting began again.

stomaching: enduring, putting up with something

not acquainting them otherwise with your full power to agree in all things: Alcibiades advised them to downplay the authority they held, saying that if the Athenians were aware of it, they would ask them for more assistance.

treat of peace: discuss peace terms

before the city of Mantinea: the Battle of Mantinea (see note)

People

Hyperbolos: or Hyperbolus; the last Athenian to be ostracized.

Thucydides: Athenian historian, author of *The Peloponnesian War*

Historic Occasions

421 B.C.: "Peace of Nicias"

420 B.C.: Athens allied with Argos, Mantinea, and Elis

418 B.C.: Battle of Mantinea

416/415 B.C.: Struggle with Hyperbolos

On the Map

Perithoedae: a *deme* (suburb) west of Athens

Pylos: a town in Messenia, in the Peloponnese peninsula

Panactum: or Panakton; a fortress in Attica

Sphacteria: a small island at the entrance to the Bay of Pylos in the Peloponnese; site of the **Battle of Sphacteria**

Elis (Elians): a region of southern Greece, on the Ionian Sea

Mantinea: or Mantineia; a city in the Peloponnese

Reading

Part One

There was a certain **Hyperbolos**, of the township of **Perithoedae**, whom **Thucydides** also speaks of as a man of bad character; a general butt for the mockery of all the comic writers of the time, but quite unconcerned at the worst things they could say; and, being careless of glory, also insensible of shame; a temper which some call boldness and courage, whereas it is indeed impudence and recklessness. He was liked by nobody; yet if the common people had any grudge to any nobleman or **magistrate**, whom they would any way accuse, Hyperbolos' wicked tongue was their instrument to utter their spite.

At this time, the people, by his persuasions, were ready to proceed to pronounce the sentence of ten years' banishment called ostracism. The manner and custom of this kind of banishment was for a time to banish out of their city such a one as seemed to have to great authority and credit in the city; and that was rather to satisfy their envy than to remedy their fear. And because it was obvious it would fall out to one of the three orators to be banished (to wit, Alcibiades, Nicias, or Phaeax): Alcibiades found means to join all their three factions in one, becoming friends one to another; and having conferred with Nicias about it, he made Hyperbolos himself to be banished, who was the chief instrument to prepare the way of their banishment. Howbeit others say, he spoke not with Nicias about it, but with Phaeax, and joining his part with Phaeax, he caused Hyperbolos to be banished, who feared nothing less: for it was never seen before, that a man of mean countenance, and of small authority, was given this banishment.

[omission for length]

Part Two

Alcibiades was not less disturbed at the distinctions which Nicias gained amongst the enemies of Athens, than at the honours which the Athenians themselves paid to him.For his house was the common inn for all Lacedaemonians when they came to Athens; moreover he had very well entertained the Lacedaemonian prisoners that were taken at **Pylos**. And afterwards **when peace was concluded** between Lacedaemon and Athens, and their prisoners redelivered home again by Nicias' means only: they loved him more than ever they did before. This was blown abroad through Greece, that the war was begun by Pericles, and that Nicias made an end of it, and the peace was generally called the "Peace of Nicias."

But Alcibiades **stomaching** this, and envying Nicias' glory, determined to break the peace whatsoever came of it. Wherefore to compass this matter, knowing first of all that the Argives had no liking of the Lacedaemonians, but were their mortal enemies, and that they did but seek matter to fall out with them: he secretly put them in hope of peace and league with the Athenians. Moreover he did persuade them to it, both by letters and word of mouth, speaking with their magistrates, and such as had greatest authority and credit amongst the people: declaring unto them that they should not fear the Lacedaemonians, nor yield to them at all, but to stick to the Athenians, who would soon repent them of the peace they had made, and break it with them.

Afterwards when the Lacedaemonians had made league with the Boeotians, and had redelivered **Panactum** to the Athenians, all defaced and spoiled, contrary to the league: Alcibiades, perceiving how the people were much offended thereat, laid hold of that opportunity to exasperate them more highly. He exclaimed fiercely against Nicias, and accused him of many things, which seemed probable enough: as that, when he was general, he made no attempt himself to capture his enemies that were shut up in the isle of **Sphacteria**, but, when they were afterwards made prisoners by others, he procured their release and sent them back to the Lacedaemonians, only to get favour with them. Also, that he would not make use of his credit with them to prevent their entering into this confederacy with the Boeotians and Corinthians, and yet, on the other side, that he sought to stand in the way of those Greeks who were inclined to make an alliance and friendship with Athens, if the Lacedaemonians did not like it.

Part Three

Now as Nicias was thus in disgrace with the people, for the causes above-said: in the midst of this stir, ambassadors came by chance from Lacedaemon to Athens, declaring that they had full powers to arrange all matters in dispute upon fair and equal terms. The council heard them and received them very courteously, and the people were to assemble the next day to give them audience: which, Alcibiades fearing much, he went secretly to confer with the ambassadors, and spoke with them apart in this sort:

> "What mean you, my lords of Sparta: do ye not know that the Senate hath always accustomed to be gracious and favourable unto those that sue unto them for any matter, and that the people contrarily are of a proud nature, and desirous to embrace all great matters? If therefore at the first sight, ye do give them to understand that you are come hither with full power, to treat freely with them in all manner of causes: do you not think that they will make you stretch your authority far, to grant them all that they will demand. Therefore, my lords ambassadors, if you look for indifference at the Athenians' hands, and that they shall not press you too far against your wills, to grant them anything of advantage: I would wish you a little to cover your full commission, and in open manner to propound certain articles and reasonable capitulations of peace, **not acquainting them otherwise with your full power to agree in all things**: and for my part, I will assure you of my goodwill in favour

of the Lacedaemonians."

When he had told them this tale, he gave them his faithful promise, and vowed as it were to perform his word. Hereupon Alcibiades turned the ambassadors from the trust they reposed in Nicias, and won them on his side: insomuch as they gave credit to no man but to him, wondering much at his great wisdom and ready wit, and they thought him a rare and notable man.

The next morning the people were assembled to give the ambassadors audience. They were sent for, and brought into the marketplace. There Alcibiades gently asked them the cause of their coming. They answered that they were come to **treat of peace**, but they had no power to determine anything. Then began Alcibiades to be angry with them, as if they had done him wrong, and not he any to them: calling them unfaithful, inconstant, and fickle men, that were come neither to do, nor say anything worth the hearing. The Senate also were offended with them, and the people rated them very roughly: whereat Nicias was so ashamed and amazed withal, that he could not tell what to say, to see so sudden a change, knowing nothing of Alcibiades' malice and subtle practice with the ambassadors.

So thus the Lacedaemonian ambassadors were utterly rejected, and Alcibiades was declared general, who presently united the Argives, the **Eleans**, and the people of **Mantinea** into a confederacy with the Athenians. Though no man did commend this practice of his, in working it after this sort: yet was it a marvellous thing of him to devise to put all Peloponnesus in arms, and to procure such a number of soldiers against the Lacedaemonians as he did **before the city of Mantinea**, and to shift of the miseries of war and hazard of battle so far from Athens. Which, if the Lacedaemonians did win, could not profit them much: and if they lost it, they could hardly save their city of Sparta.

[omission for length]

Narration and Discussion

Explain how Alcibiades deceived the Spartan ambassadors. What was the result?

Creative narration: Write or act out a scene in which Alcibiades raises his accusations against Nicias. How might Nicias respond?

Creative narration for older students: Create a scene where Alcibiades visits his old friend Socrates. You might imagine particularly that Socrates brings up the rather sore subject of Nicias. What advice might he give?

Lesson Five

Introduction

The first part of this lesson gives further examples of the eccentricities of Alcibiades, including his fancy purple robes and his refusal to sleep on a hard ship's bed. According to Plutarch, the Athenians seemed to regard him as inconvenient and expensive, but useful.

The second part describes the Athenian plan to take over the island of Sicily, which Alcibiades enthusiastically promoted. Nicias protested that such an expedition would take a huge budget and a great number of ships. To his annoyance, the Athenian council became excited about the idea, and Nicias himself was chosen as general for the expedition.

Vocabulary

exorbitant luxury and wantonness: extravagance; lack of restraint in spending money and also in behaviour.

abide: Dryden uses the word "support." We might say "afford."

girths: straps

contemn: hold in contempt, disdain

being manifest tokens…: showing that he was extremely ambitious

abhors: hates, finds disgusting

rule the roost: The expression "rule the roost" has been used since the 15th century to describe someone who bosses others around.

liberalities: generosity

reviled: jeered at, insulted

sundry: varying

succour: aid

furnish them with victuals: supply them with food

his companion and associate: that is, Alcibiades

People

Aglauros: or Agraulos or Aglaurus; the mythical daughter of Cecrops (the first Athenian king), who had a temple dedicated to her on the Acropolis. Young soldiers, on receiving their first suit of armour, swore an oath to her to defend their city to the last.

Aristophanes: famous Athenian playwright

Archestratus: a poet known for his writings on food

Timon the Misanthrope: a citizen of Athens known for his dislike or of people; the inspiration for Shakespeare's play *Timon of Athens*

Lamachus: the third general in the **Sicilian Expedition**; honoured in Aristophanes' play *The Frogs*.

Historic Occasions

415-413 B.C.: Sicilian Expedition

On the Map

Sicily: large island at the tip of mainland Italy. It was strategically important because it was close to wealthy North African cities such as Carthage.

Syracuse (Syracusans): a colony and city on the island of **Sicily**, founded by the Corinthians

Reading

Part One

Now although Alcibiades did make the city of Athens strong by sea, yet he did not neglect to persuade the Athenians also to make themselves strong by land. For he did put the young men oftentimes in mind of the oath they were made to swear to **Aglauros**, to the effect that they would account wheat and barley, and vines and olives, to be the limits of **Attica**; by which they were taught to claim a title to all land that was cultivated and productive.

Yet with all these goodly deeds and fair words of Alcibiades, and with this great courage and quickness of understanding, he had many great faults and imperfections. He intermingled **exorbitant luxury and wantonness**, in his eating and drinking *[North: "riotous banquets"]* and dissolute living; wore long purple robes which dragged after him as he went through the marketplace; caused the planks of his galley to be cut away, so that he might lie the softer, his bed not being placed on the boards, but hanging upon **girths**. His shield, again, which was richly gilded, had not the usual ensigns of the Athenians; but a Cupid, holding a thunderbolt in his hand, was painted upon it.

The noblemen and best citizens of Athens perceiving this, they were much offended at him, but were afraid withal of his rashness and insolence: he did so **contemn** the laws and customs of their country, **being manifest tokens of a man that aspired to be king**, and would subvert and turn all overhand. And as for the goodwill of the common people towards him, the poet **Aristophanes** doth plainly express it in these words:

> The people most desire what most they hate to have:
>
> and what their mind **abhors**, even that they seem to crave.

And in another place he said also, aggravating the suspicion they had of him:

> For state or commonwealth, much better should it be,
>
> to keep within the country none such lion's looks as he.
>
> But if they needs will keep, a lion to their cost,

then must they needs obey his will, for he will rule the
roost.

For to say truly: his courtesies, his **liberalities**, and noble expenses to show the people so great pleasure and pastime as nothing could be more; the glorious memory of his ancestors, the grace of his eloquence, the beauty of his person, the strength and valiantness of his body, joined together with his wisdom and experience in martial affairs, were the very causes that made them to bear with him in all things, and that the Athenians did patiently endure all his excesses, and did cover his faults with the best words and terms they could, calling them "youthful," and "gentlemen's sports." As when he kept Agartharchus the painter prisoner in his house by force, until he had painted all his walls within: and when he had done, did let him go, and rewarded him very honestly for his pains. He publicly struck Taureas, who exhibited certain shows in opposition to him and contended with him for the prize. *[omission for content]* Wherefore it seemed **Archestratus'** words were spoken to good purpose, when he said that Greece could not **abide** two Alcibiades at once.

Once, when Alcibiades succeeded well in an oration which he made, and the whole assembly attended upon him to do him honour, **Timon the Misanthrope** did not pass slightly by him, nor avoid him, as did others, but purposely met him, and taking him by the hand, said, "Go on boldly, my son, and increase in credit with the people; for thou wilt one day bring them calamities enough." When they had heard these words, those that stood by fell a-laughing. Others **reviled** Timon; others again marked well his words, and thought of them many a time after; such **sundry** opinions they had of Alcibiades for the inconstancy of his life, and waywardness of his nature and conditions.

Part Two

The Athenians, even in the lifetime of Pericles, had already cast a longing eye upon Sicily; but did not attempt anything till after his death. Then, under pretense of aiding their confederates, they sent **succour** upon all occasions to those who were oppressed by the **Syracusans**, preparing the way for sending over a greater force. But Alcibiades was the person who inflamed this desire of theirs to the height, so that, upon his persuasions, they built castles in the air, and thought to do great wonders only by their winning of Sicily. But that was to Alcibiades but a beginning of further enterprises.

Nicias endeavoured to divert the people from the expedition by representing to them that the taking of Syracuse would be a work of great difficulty; but Alcibiades dreamed of nothing less than the conquest of Carthage and Libya, and by the accession of these conceiving himself at once made master of Italy and Peloponnesus, seemed to look upon Sicily as only to **furnish them with victuals**, and to pay the soldiers for their conquests which he had imagined. The young men were soon elevated with these hopes, and listened gladly to those of riper years, who talked wonders of the countries they were going to, so that you might see great numbers sitting in the wrestling grounds and public places, drawing on the ground the figure of the island and the situation of Libya and Carthage.

[omission for length]

But Nicias, against his will, was chosen captain, to take charge of men in these wars. He misliked this journey as well for **his companion and associate** in the charge of these wars, as for other misfortunes he foresaw therein. Howbeit the Athenians thought the war would fall out well if they did not commit it wholly to Alcibiades' rashness and hardiness, but did join with him the wisdom of Nicias; and they appointed **Lamachus** also for their third captain, whom they sent thither, though he were waxen now somewhat old, as one that had showed himself no less venturous and hardy in some battles than Alcibiades himself.

Narration and Discussion

Why were the Athenians so willing to put up with Alcibiades' excesses?

"Wherefore it seemed Archestratus' words were spoken to good purpose, when he said that Greece could not abide two Alcibiades at once." Dryden translates it "that Greece could not support a second Alcibiades." Why not?

Creative narration #1: Write or act out a conversation about the choice of a general for the Sicilian Expedition.

Creative narration #2: Those familiar with *The Sound of Music* will remember the song "How Do You Solve a Problem Like Maria?" in which a group of nuns sing about her good and bad points. Those with a musical bent might want to write a similar song about Alcibiades.

Lesson Six

Introduction

At this point things took an unexpected turn, as Alcibiades was called back from the campaign in Sicily almost before it had begun, to answer certain criminal charges which he thought had been put aside for the sake of the expedition. It seemed that, in his absence, the whole matter had been stirred up again, and he would now have to stand trial for his alleged blasphemies.

However, Alcibiades had no intention of complying, and he escaped into mainland Italy.

Vocabulary

the furniture and order of these wars: what they would need and how they would organize things

thwart: block

levy: collect, register

at their discretion: as they thought best

in the neck one of another: right after one another

hacked and hewed: cut, as if by axes or swords

toys: small things

lewd: offensive

first founders of them: Corinth founded the colony of Syracuse

demagogues: political leaders who play on the desires of the people

profanely acted: Alcibiades and his friends were accused of mocking religious rites during a party.

fetch: trick

could not persuade them: that is, to give him a fair trial then and there

sedition: rebellion

People

Androcles: an orator who accused Alcibiades of ruining sacred images

On the Map

Rhegium: a city on the toe of Italy's "boot," across from Sicily

Catana: a city in Sicily

Reading

Part One

Now when they came to resolve of the number of soldiers, **the furniture and order of these wars**, Nicias sought crookedly to **thwart** this journey, and to break it off altogether: but Alcibiades withstood him, and got the better hand of him. There was an orator called Demostratus, who moved the people also that the captains whom they had chosen for these wars might have full power and authority to **levy** men **at their discretion**, and to make such preparation as they thought good: whereunto the people agreed, and did authorize them. But when they were even ready to go their way, many signs of ill success lighted **in the neck one of another**; and, amongst the rest, this was one. That they were commanded to take ship on the day of the celebration of the Feast of Adonia, on which the custom is that women do set up in divers places of the city, in the midst of the streets, images like to dead corpses, which they carry to burial, and they represent the mourning and lamentations made at the funerals of the dead, with blubbering and beating themselves, in token of the sorrow the goddess Venus made for the death of her friend Adonis. Moreover, the Hermes (which are the images of Mercury, and were wont to be set up in every lane and street) were found in a night all **hacked and hewed**, and mangled specially in their faces: but this put divers in great fear and trouble, yea even those that made no account of such **toys**. Whereupon it was alleged that it might be the Corinthians that did it, or procured that **lewd** act to be done, favouring the Syracusans, who were their near kinsmen, and had been the **first founders of them**; imagining upon this ill token, it might be a cause to break off the enterprise, and to make the people repent them that they had taken this war in hand.

Nevertheless, the people would not allow this excuse; neither would they hearken to those that said they should not reckon of any such signs or tokens, and that they were but some light-brained youths, that, being drunk, had played this shameful part in their bravery, or for sport. But they took these signs very grievously, and were indeed not a little afraid, looking upon it to proceed from a conspiracy of persons who designed some commotions in the state. The council, as well as the assembly of the people, which were held frequently in a few days' space, examined diligently everything that might administer grounds for suspicion.

Now whilst they were busily searching out the matter, **Androcles**, one of the **demagogues**, brought before the council certain slaves and strangers that dwelt in Athens, who insisted that Alcibiades, and others of his friends and companions, had hacked and mangled other images after that sort; and had **profanely acted** also, at a banquet, the Ceremonies of the Holy Mysteries.

[omission for length]

Whereat the people being marvellously moved and offended, and the orator Androcles, his mortal enemy, aggravating and stirring them up the more against him: Alcibiades, a little at the first, began to be amazed at it. But afterwards, hearing that the mariners which were prepared for the voyage to Sicily, and the soldiers also that were gathered, did bear him great goodwill, and specially how the aid, and that band that came from Argos and Mantinea (being a thousand footmen, well-armed and appointed) did say openly how it was for Alcibiades' sake they did take upon them so long a voyage beyond sea, and that if they went about to do him any hurt or wrong, they would presently return home again from whence they came: he began to be of a good courage again, and determined, with this good favourable opportunity of time, to come before the council, to answer to all such articles and accusations as should be laid against him.

[Omission for length: certain people were persuaded to speak in favour of letting Alcibiades go off and fight, and have his trial later. Alcibiades protested, saying that he could not fight well with such accusations hanging over his head.]

But all this **could not persuade them**. Thus he was compelled to take the seas with his other companions, having in their navy about a hundred and forty galleys, all having three oars to a bank; and five thousand one hundred footmen very well armed and appointed, and throwers with slings, archers, and other light armed men to the number of thirteen hundred, sufficiently furnished of all warlike and necessary munition.

Part Two

Now after they were arrived on the coast of Italy, they landed at **Rhegium**: where, holding counsel in what sort they should direct these wars, Alcibiades was opposed by Nicias; but Lamachus being of his opinion, they sailed for Sicily forthwith, and took **Catana**. But he never did any exploit after that, for he was called home immediately, by the Athenians, to come and answer certain accusations.

For as we told you before, there was at the beginning certain light suspicions and accusations put up against him, by some slaves and strangers. And that afterwards his enemies in Athens enforced those accusations, and burdened him more cruelly, adding to his former fault that he had "broken the images of Mercury, and had committed sacrilege in counterfeiting in jest and mockery the holy Ceremonies of the Mysteries"; and blew into the ears of the people that both the one and the other were intended to change and alter the government of the state of the city.

Upon this information, the people took it in so ill part, that they committed all those to prison that were in any sort accused or suspected thereof, and would never let them come to their answer: and moreover did much repent them that they had not condemned Alcibiades, upon so great accusations as were exhibited against him, while his offense was in question before them.

[An orator named Andocides unexpectedly confessed to the crime of damaging the statues, and this was expected to end the matter.]

Now though the people had no more occasion to occupy their busy heads about the breakers of these images, yet was not their malice thus appeased against Alcibiades, until they sent the galley called the *Salaminian*, commanding those they sent by a special commission to seek him out; in no case to attempt to take him by force, nor to lay hold on him by violence; but to use him with all the good words and courteous manner that they possibly could, and to will him only to appear in person before the people, to answer to certain accusations put up against him.

[omission for length: a written complaint, giving details of the blasphemous acts supposedly committed by Alcibiades]

If otherwise they should have used force, they feared much lest the army would have mutinied on his behalf within the country of their enemies, and that there would have grown some **sedition** amongst their soldiers. This might Alcibiades have easily done, if he had been disposed. For the soldiers were very sorry to see him depart, perceiving that the wars should be drawn out now in length, and be much prolonged under Nicias, seeing Alcibiades was taken from them, who was the only spur that pricked Nicias forward to do any service; and that Lamachus also, though he were a valiant man, yet he lacked honour and authority in the army, because he was but a mean man born, and poor besides.

Narration and Discussion

In a previous lesson, we read that the Athenians were generally willing to put up with Alcibiades' excesses, because they recognized that he could be a good leader, particularly when it came to military strategy. What changed their minds?

Creative narration: If you are working with a group, this lesson lends itself to drama and/or debate. (Do you think Alcibiades was guilty?)

Lesson Seven

Introduction

Alcibiades knew it would be dangerous for him to return to Athens. He escaped to Sparta and started acting like a Spartan. An excellent Spartan, a fantastic Spartan. Was it all outward appearance?

Vocabulary

contumacious: willfully disobedient

black broth: a Spartan dish believed to have been made of pigs' blood, salt, and vinegar

satrap: governor who was subject to a king or overlord

pomp and sumptuousness: rich lifestyle

he went unto Tissaphernes: Alcibiades crossed into Persia

guile: deceitfulness

salubrious: health-giving, pleasant

diminish and consume: waste away

People

Tissaphernes: Persian statesman, satrap of Lydia

Lycurgus: legendary founder of the Spartan way of life

Pharnabazus: Pharnabazus II;, satrap of Lesser Phrygia

King Agis: Agis II of Sparta

Gylippus: Spartan (Lacedaemonian) captain

Historic Occasions

415 B.C.: Alcibiades escaped to Sparta

414/413 B.C.: The second half of the Peloponnesian War began

413 B.C.: Nicias was captured and executed by Spartan allies

412 B.C.: The Persians captured most of Ionia

412 B.C.: Alcibiades tried his luck with the Persians

On the Map

Messena: or Messina; a city in Sicily

Thurii: a city on the Tarentine Gulf in southern Italy

Decelea: a *deme* and village in northern Attica, located along a trade route which connected Athens to Euboea

Cyzicus: a town of the region of Mysia

Reading

Part One

Now Alcibiades, just upon his departure, prevented **Messena** from falling into the hands of the Athenians. There were some in that city who were upon the point of delivering it up; but he, knowing the persons, gave information to some friends of the Syracusans, and so defeated the whole contrivance.

When he arrived at **Thurii**, he went on shore, and, concealing himself there, escaped those who searched after him. Yet there was one that knew him where he was, and said: "Why, how now Alcibiades, dost not thou trust the justice of thy country?" "Yes, very well," quoth he, "if it were in another matter: but my life standing upon it, I would not trust mine own mother, fearing lest negligently she should put in the black bean, where she should cast in the white." For by the first, condemnation of death was signified: and by the other, pardon of life. But afterwards, hearing that the Athenians for malice had condemned him to death: "Well," quoth he, "they shall know I am yet alive."

He was condemned as **contumacious** upon his not appearing; his property was confiscated; and it was decreed that all the priests and priestesses should solemnly curse him.

[omission for length]

Part Two

After this most grievous sentence and condemnation passed against him, Alcibiades departed out of Thurii, and went into the Peloponnesus, where he remained some time at Argos. But in the end, fearing his enemies, and having no hope to return again to his own country with any safety, he sent to Sparta, desiring safe conduct, and assuring them that he would make them amends by his future services for all the mischief he had done them while he was their enemy.

The Spartans giving him the security he desired, he went eagerly, was well received, at his very first coming, succeeded in inducing them, without any further caution or delay, to send aid to the Syracusans. He so roused and excited them, that they forthwith dispatched Gylippus into Sicily, to crush the forces which the Athenians had there. A second point was to renew the war upon the Athenians at home. But the third thing, and the most important of all, was to make them fortify **Decelea**, which above everything reduced and wasted the resources of the Athenians.

The renown which he earned by these "public services" was equaled by the admiration he attracted to his private life. He captivated and won over everybody by his conformity to Spartan habits. People who saw him wearing his hair close cut, bathing in cold water, eating coarse meal, and dining on **black broth**, doubted, or rather could not believe, that he ever had a cook in his house, or had ever seen a perfumer, or had worn a mantle of Milesian purple.

For he had, as it was observed, this peculiar talent and artifice for gaining men's affections, that he could at once comply with, embrace, and enter into their habits and ways of life, and change faster than the chameleon. One colour, indeed, they say the chameleon cannot assume: it cannot itself appear white; but Alcibiades, whether with good men or with bad, could adapt himself to his company, as well the good as the bad.

At Sparta, he was devoted to athletic exercises, was frugal and reserved. In Ionia, to the contrary: there he lived daintily and superfluously, and gave himself to all mirth and pleasure. In Thrace, he drank ever, or was always a-horseback. If he came to Tissaphernes, satrap of the mighty king of Persia, he far exceeded the magnificence of Persia in **pomp and sumptuousness**. And these things, notwithstanding, never altered his natural condition from one fashion to another, neither did his manners (to say truly) receive all sorts of changes. But because peradventure, if he had showed his natural disposition, he might in divers places where he came, have offended those whose company he kept, he transformed himself into any shape, and adopted any fashion, that he observed to be most agreeable to him.

Sidebar

Alcibiades fathered a child by the wife of **King Agis** of Sparta, while Agis was away fighting. He excused himself by saying that he "had not done this thing out of mere wantonness of insult, nor to gratify a passion, but that his race might one day be kings over the Lacedaemonians."

Part Three

After the defeat which the Athenians received in Sicily, ambassadors were dispatched to Sparta at once from Chios and Lesbos and **Cyzicus**, to signify their purpose of revolting from the Athenians. The Boeotians favoured those of Lesbos; **Pharnabazus** favoured the Cyzicenes; but the Lacedaemonians, at the persuasion of Alcibiades, chose to assist Chios before all others. He himself, also, went instantly to sea, procured the immediate revolt of almost all Ionia, and, co-operating with the Lacedaemonian generals, did great mischief to the

Athenians.

But Agis was his enemy, hating him for having dishonoured his wife, and also impatient of his glory, as almost every enterprise and every success was ascribed to Alcibiades. Others also of the greatest authority among the Spartans, that were most ambitious among them, began in their minds to be angry with Alcibiades, for the envy they bore him: who were of so great power, that they procured their governors to write their letters to their captains in the field, to kill him. Alcibiades, hearing of this, did no whit desist to do all he could for the benefit of the Lacedaemonians: yet he had an eye behind him, fleeing all occasions to fall into their hands.

So in the end, for more surety of his person, **he went unto Tissaphernes**, the king of Persia's satrap; and immediately became the first and most influential person about him. For this barbarous man, not being himself sincere, but a lover of **guile** and wickedness, admired his cleverness. And, indeed, the charm of daily interaction with him was more than any character could resist or any disposition escape. Even those who feared and envied him could not but take delight, and have a sort of kindness for him, when they saw him and were in his company. So that Tissaphernes, otherwise a cruel character, and above all other Persians, a hater of the Greeks, was yet so won by the flatteries of Alcibiades that he set himself even to exceed him in responding to them. The most beautiful of his parks, containing **salubrious** streams and meadows, where he had built pavilions, and places of retirement royally and exquisitely adorned, received by his direction the name of "Alcibiades," and was always so called and so spoken of.

Alcibiades despairing utterly to find any safety or friendship among the Spartans, and fearing on the other side King Agis also: he began to speak ill of them, and to disgrace all that they did, to Tissaphernes. By this practice he stayed Tissaphernes from aiding them so friendly as he might: moreover, he did not utterly destroy the Athenians. For he persuaded him that he should furnish the Lacedaemonians but with little money, to let them **diminish and consume** by little and little: to the end that after one had troubled and weakened the other, they both at the length should be the easier for the king to overcome.

This barbarous man did easily consent to this device. All the world then saw he loved Alcibiades, and esteemed him very much, in the same way as he was well regarded by the Greeks on both sides. Then were the Athenians sorry, and repented, when they had received so great loss and hurt, for that they had decreed so severely against Alcibiades, who in like manner was very sorrowful to see them brought to so hard terms, fearing if the city of Athens came to destruction, that he himself should fall in the end into the hands of the Lacedaemonians, who maliced him to the death.

Narration and Discussion

How did Alcibiades change during his exile in Sparta? How did he stay the same?

Why did Alcibiades decide suddenly that it would be a better idea to live among the Persians?

Why did Tissaphernes find Alcibiades an intriguing character?

Creative narration #1: Alcibiades has delegated you to be his "Spartan lifestyle coach." Write or act out your advice for him; perhaps have him sample some (simulated) black broth.

Creative narration #2: You are a reporter who has been granted an exclusive interview with Tissaphernes, perhaps in "Alcibiades Park." What questions will you ask?

Lesson Eight

Introduction

Although Alcibiades was not pleased about the way his city had treated him, he worried that if Athens lost the war, he would then be at the mercy of Sparta, and particularly King Agis, who carried a personal grudge against him. He decided to do whatever he could to avoid that happening.

At this point, the scheming and double-dealing got very complicated. But in the end, strangely enough, Alcibiades was invited not only to lead the navy, but to return home.

Vocabulary

inveighed: spoke in opposition, with hostility

prevailed: were successful, got what they wanted

slighted: snubbed, ignored

unequivocally: unquestionably

People

Phrynichus, Pisander: leaders of the Four Hundred

Astyochus: Spartan (Lacedaemonian) admiral

Thrasybulus of Steiria (#1): Athenian general and civic leader

Historic Occasions

411 B.C.: The Athenian government was replaced by the Four Hundred

411 B.C.: Alcibiades was made general of the Athenian military forces

On the Map

Samos: an island in the eastern Aegean Sea

Piraeus: the harbour very close to Athens

Hellespont: also called the Dardanelles; part of the strait that divides Europe from Asia (along with the **Bosphorus**). The word is sometimes used to refer to the region around it.

Aspendos: or Aspendus; a city in Pamphylia, Asia Minor

Reading

Part One

At that time, the whole strength of the Athenians was in **Samos.** Their fleet maintained itself here, and issued from these headquarters to reduce such as had revolted, and protect the rest of their territories; in one way or other still contriving to be a match for their enemies at sea. What they stood in fear of was Tissaphernes, and the Phoenician fleet of one hundred and fifty galleys, which was said to be already under sail; if those came, there remained then no hopes for the commonwealth of Athens.

Understanding this, Alcibiades sent secretly unto the chiefest men that were in the army of the Athenians at Samos, to give them hope he would make Tissaphernes their friend: howbeit not of any desire he had to gratify the people, nor that he trusted to the commonalty of Athens, but only to the "honourable and honest citizens," and that conditionally so as they had the heart and courage to bridle a little the insolence of the people; and, by taking upon them the government, would endeavour to save the city from ruin. All the heads and chief men did give very good ear unto it: saving only **Phrynichus**, of the township of Dirades, one of the generals; who suspected, as the truth was, that Alcibiades concerned not himself whether the government were in the common people or the "better" citizens, but that he only sought by any means to make way for his return into his native country; and to that end **inveighed** against the people, thereby to gain the others, and to insinuate himself into their good opinion.

But when Phrynichus found his counsel to be rejected and that he was himself become a declared enemy of Alcibiades, he gave secret information to **Astyochus**, then admiral to the Lacedaemonians, of Alcibiades' practice; and warned him to take heed of him, and to lay him up safe as a double-dealer, and one that had intelligence with both sides; but he understood not how it was but one traitor to speak to another. For this Astyochus was eager to gain the favour of Tissaphernes, observing the credit Alcibiades had with him; and he revealed to Alcibiades all that Phrynichus had said against him.

Alcibiades straight sent men to Samos, unto the captains there, to accuse Phrynichus of the treason he had revealed against them. Those of the council there, receiving this intelligence, were highly offended with Phrynichus.

So Phrynichus, seeing no better way to save himself for making of this fault, went about to make amends with committing a worse fault. He sent again to Astyochus to reproach him for betraying him; and to make an offer to him at the same time to deliver into his hands both the army and the navy of the Athenians. Howbeit this treason of Phrynichus did the Athenians no hurt at all, by reason of Astyochus' counter-treason: for he did let Alcibiades again understand what offer Phrynichus had made him. But this again was foreseen by Phrynichus, who, expecting a second accusation from Alcibiades, to anticipate him, advertised the Athenians beforehand that the enemy was ready to sail in order to surprise them; and therefore advised them to fortify their camp, and be in a readiness to go aboard their ships.

While the Athenians were intent upon doing these things, they received other letters from Alcibiades, admonishing them to beware of Phrynichus, as one who designed to betray their fleet to the enemy; to which they gave no credit at all, conceiving that Alcibiades, who knew perfectly the counsels and preparations of the enemy, was merely making use of that knowledge in order to impose upon them in this false accusation of Phrynichus. (Yet, afterwards, when Phrynichus was stabbed by a dagger in the marketplace by Hermon, one of the guards, the Athenians, entering into an examination of the cause, solemnly condemned Phrynichus of treason, and decreed crowns to Hermon and his associates.)

Part Two

Those that were Alcibiades' friends, being at that time the greatest men of the council in the army at Samos, sent one **Pisander** to Athens, to attempt to alter the government, and to encourage the noblemen to take upon them the authority, and to pluck it from the people. They assured them that Tissaphernes would give them aid to do it, by means of Alcibiades, who would make him their friend. This was the colour and cloak wherewith they served their turns, that did change the government of Athens, and that brought it into the hands of a small number of nobility.

But as soon as they **prevailed**, and had got the administration of affairs into their hands, under the name of the Five Thousand (whereas, indeed, they were but Four Hundred), they **slighted** Alcibiades altogether, and prosecuted the war with less vigour; partly because they dared not yet trust the citizens, who secretly detested this change; and partly also because they were of opinion that the

Lacedaemonians (who at all times did most favour the government of nobility) would be better inclined to make peace with them.

Part Three

Now the common people that remained still in the city stirred not, but were quiet against their wills, for fear of danger, because there were many of them slain that boldly took upon them in open presence to resist these four hundred. But those who were at Samos, indignant when they heard this news, were eager to set sail instantly for the **Piraeus**; sending for Alcibiades, they declared him general, requiring him to lead them on to put down the tyrants.

He, however, in that juncture, did not, as it might have been thought a man would, on being suddenly exalted by the favour of a multitude, think himself under an obligation to gratify and submit to all the wishes of those who, from a fugitive and an exile, had created him general of so great an army, and given him the command of such a fleet. But to the contrary, as it became a general worthy of such a charge, he considered with himself that it was his part wisely to stay those who would in a rage and fury carelessly cast themselves away, and not suffer them to do it. And by restraining them from the great error they were about to commit, he **unequivocally** saved the commonwealth. For if they then sailed to Athens, all Ionia, and the islands, and the **Hellespont** would have fallen into the enemies' hands without opposition; while the Athenians, involved in civil war, would have been fighting with one another within the circuit of their own walls.

It was Alcibiades alone, or, at least, principally, who prevented all this mischief; not only by persuading the whole army, and declaring the inconvenience thereof, which would fall out upon their sudden departure: but also by entreating some, and constraining others. He was much assisted, however, by **Thrasybulus of Steiria (#1)**, who went along with him, and cried out to those who were ready to be gone. For he had the biggest and loudest voice as they say, of any man that was in all the city of Athens.

A second great service which Alcibiades did for them was his undertaking that the Phoenician fleet, which the Lacedaemonians expected to be sent to them by the king of Persia, should either come in aid of the Athenians or otherwise should not come at all. For he departed immediately, and went with great speed to Tissaphernes: whom he handled in such sort, that he brought not the ships that lay at rode before the city of **Aspendos**, and so he broke promise with the Lacedaemonians. Therefore Alcibiades was marvellously blamed and accused, both by the one and the other side, to have altered Tissaphernes' mind; but chiefly by the Lacedaemonians, who said that he had persuaded this barbarous captain that he should neither aid the one nor the other, but rather to suffer them one to devour and destroy each other. For it was evident that the accession of so great a force to either party would enable them to take away the entire dominion of the sea from the other side.

Shortly after, the four hundred usurpers were driven out, the friends of Alcibiades vigorously assisting those who were for the popular government. And now the people in the city not only desired, but commanded Alcibiades to return home from exile. But he judged with himself it would be of no honour nor grace unto him to return as only upon the people's favour and goodwill; whereas if he had done some greater exploit, his return might be both glorious and triumphant.

[Omission for length: the "exploit" Alcibiades took on was a successful sea battle against the Lacedaemonians.]

Narration and Discussion

Explain how Alcibiades moved so quickly from being a fugitive to being general of the Athenian forces.

Creative narration: Explain the events with Phrynichus in any way that makes sense: a series of news headlines, or messages sent between two people.

Lesson Nine

Introduction

Alcibiades had a short setback when his "friend" Tissaphernes put

Alcibiades under house arrest (to please the king, with whom he needed to score points). However, Alcibiades managed to escape, and got revenge by telling everyone that Tissaphernes had helped him to do so.

With that out of the way, he sailed to the Athenian camp, and used his eloquence so well with the soldiers there that they immediately sailed off with him to attack the harbour of Cyzicus, in an attempt to control the Hellespont (an important water gateway).

And then it was time for Alcibiades to return to Athens. Would he be welcomed as a hero, or arrested as a criminal?

Vocabulary

entertainment: friendly treatment, welcome

defamed: slandered; talked about badly

in very happy hour: at exactly the right time

discharge and purge him to the king: put him in the king's good books again

professing he was a party to his escape: telling everyone that Tissaphernes had helped him escape

must be all one for them: they must do all those things

ephors: Spartan city leaders

their short laconic manner: The Spartans were famous for saying everything in the fewest possible words.

invincible: unconquerable

extol: praise

routed: defeated

seignory: power; position of command

suburbs: outlying districts of the city

so turmoiled with civil dissension: in such a mess from riots and fighting within the city

People

Thrasyllus: Athenian general known for his part in the Peloponnesian War

Historic Occasions

410 B.C.: The Battle of Cyzicus

409-408 B.C.: Siege of Byzantium

409 B.C.: Defeat of Thrasyllus near Ephesus

408 B.C.: The Athenians retook Chalcedon, Byzantium, and other cities in the Hellespont

Somewhere between 410 B.C. and 407 B.C.: Alcibiades' return to Athens

On the Map

Sardis: the capital city of the kingdom of **Lydia**

Clazomenae: city on the coast of Ionia

Isle of Proconnesus: or Marmara Island, in the Sea of Marmara

Abydos: a city of Mysia

Chalcedon: a town of Bithynia, in Asia Minor

Reading

Part One

Alcibiades, having now happily gotten this glorious victory, would needs go show himself in triumph unto Tissaphernes. So having prepared to present him with goodly rich presents, and appointed also a convenient train and number of sail meet for a general, he took his course directly to him. But he found not that **entertainment** he hoped for. For Tissaphernes, standing in great hazard of displeasure, and fear of punishment at the king's hands; and having long time before been **defamed** by the Lacedaemonians, who had complained of him that he did not fulfill the king's commandment; thought that Alcibiades was arrived **in very happy hour**; whereupon he kept him prisoner in the city of **Sardis**, supposing the wrong he had done would by this means easily **discharge and purge him to the king**.

But about thirty days after, Alcibiades escaped from his keeping; and, having got a horse, fled to **Clazomenae**, where he procured Tissaphernes additional disgrace by **professing he was a party to his escape**.

Part Two

From there he sailed to the Athenian camp, and, being informed there that Mindarus and Pharnabazus were together at Cyzicus, he made a speech to the soldiers, telling them that sea-fighting, land-fighting, and, by the gods, fighting against fortified cities too, **must be all one for them**; as unless they conquered everywhere, there was no money for them.

His oration ended, he made them immediately hoist sail, and so to go lie at anchor in the **Isle of Proconnesus**: where he took order that they should seize all the small vessels they met, and guard them safely in the interior of the fleet, so that the enemy might have no notice of his coming. A great storm of rain, accompanied with thunder and darkness, which happened at the same time, contributed much to the concealment of his enterprise. Indeed, it was not only undiscovered by the enemy, but the Athenians themselves were ignorant of it; for he commanded them suddenly on board, and set sail when they had abandoned all intention of it.

As the darkness presently passed away, the Peloponnesian fleet was seen riding out at sea, in front of the harbour of Cyzicus. Fearing that if they discovered the number of his ships, they might endeavour to save themselves by land, he commanded the rest of the captains to slacken, and follow him slowly; whilst he, advancing with forty ships, showed himself to the enemy, and provoked them to fight.

The enemy, supposing there had been no more ships than those that were in sight, did set out presently to fight with them. They were no sooner joined together, but Alcibiades' ships that came behind were also seen approaching: the enemies were so terrified that they fled immediately.

Upon that, Alcibiades, breaking through the midst of them with twenty of his best ships, hastened to the shore, disembarked, and pursued those who abandoned their ships and fled to land, and made a great slaughter of them. Moreover, Mindarus, and Pharnabazus, being come out of the city to rescue their people, were overthrown both. He slew Mindarus in the field, fighting valiantly: as for Pharnabazus, he cowardly fled away. So the Athenians spoiled the dead bodies (which were a great number) of a great deal of armour and riches, and took besides all their enemies' ships.

They also made themselves masters of Cyzicus, which was deserted by Pharnabazus, and destroyed its Peloponnesian garrison; and thereby not only secured to themselves the Hellespont, but by force drove the Lacedaemonians from out of all the rest of the sea. They intercepted some letters written to the **ephors**, which gave an account of this fatal overthrow, after **their short laconic manner**. "Our hopes are at an end. Mindarus is slain. The men starve. We know not what to do."

Part Three

The soldiers who followed Alcibiades in this last fight were so exalted with their success, and felt that degree of pride, that, looking on themselves as **invincible**, they disdained to mix with the older soldiers, who had been often overcome. A little before this happened, forces led by **Thrasyllus** had been overthrown by the city of Ephesus. And for this overthrow, the Ephesians had set up a brass trophy to the disgrace of the Athenians. For the which Alcibiades' soldiers did very much rebuke Thrasyllus' men, and did exceedingly **extol** their captain and themselves, and would neither encamp with them, neither have to do with them, nor yet keep them company. But soon after, Pharnabazus, with a great force of cavalry and foot soldiers, fell upon the soldiers of Thrasyllus, as they were laying waste the territory of

Abydos. Alcibiades came to their aid, **routed** Pharnabazus, and together with Thrasyllus pursued him till it was night; and in this action the troops united, and returned together to the camp, rejoicing and congratulating one another.

The next morning Alcibiades set up a triumph for the victory he had the day before; and then went to spoil and destroy Pharnabazus' country; and no man dared once come out to meet him.

[*omission for length*]

Part Four

Alcibiades laid siege to the city of **Chalcedon**, which he environed all about from the one side of the sea to the other. Pharnabazus came thither, thinking to have raised the siege. And Hippocrates, a captain of the Lacedaemonians, that was governor of the city, assembled all the force he was able to make within the same, and made a sally out also upon the Athenians at the very same time. Whereupon Alcibiades putting his men in order of battle, so as they might give a charge upon them both at one instant: he fought so valiantly, that he forced Pharnabazus to run his way with shame enough, and slew Hippocrates in the field, with a great number of his men.

[Omission for length: Alcibiades also attacked Selymbria and Byzantium.]

Part Five

Now Alcibiades desirous in the end to see his native country again (or to speak more truly, that his countrymen should see him) after he had so many times overthrown their enemies in battle: he hoisted sail, and directed his course towards Athens, bringing with him all the galleys of the Athenians richly furnished, and decked all about with armour and weapons gotten amongst the spoils of his enemies.

[Omission for length: Plutarch points out that, although Alcibiades arrived in great splendour, he must have had certain doubts about his welcome.]

He was no sooner landed, but all the people ran out of every corner to see him, with so great love and affection, that they took no heed of the other captains that came with him, but clustered all to him only, and cried out for joy to see him. Those that could come near him, did welcome and embrace him: but all the people wholly followed him. And some that came to him, put garlands of flowers upon his head: and those that could not come near him, saw him afar off, and the old folks did point him out to the younger sort.

But this common joy was mingled, notwithstanding, with tears and sorrow, when they came to think upon their former misfortunes and calamities, and to compare them with their present prosperity: weighing with themselves also how they would not have lost Sicily, nor would their hope in all things else have failed them, if they had delivered themselves and the charge of their army into Alcibiades' hands, when they sent for him to appear in person before them.

Considering also how he found the city of Athens in manner put from their **seigniory** and commandment on the sea, and on the other side how their force by land was brought unto such extremity that Athens scantly could defend her **suburbs**, the city itself being **so turmoiled with civil dissension**: yet he gathered together that small force that remained, and had now not only restored Athens to her former power and sovereignty on the sea, but had made her also a conqueror by land.

Narration and Discussion

Pretend you are with someone who is visiting and does not know what the excitement is about. How will you explain it to them?

Since Alcibiades' homecoming was so successful, what might his ambition now lead him to expect from the Athenians? Do you think he will get what he wants?

Creative narration for older students: You are an Athenian playwright, and you want to work the return of Alcibiades into your new comedy. Write a few lines of verse to mark the occasion.

Lesson Ten

Introduction

Now that Alcibiades was finally home (if only for a short time), he looked around for projects that could boost his popularity with the Athenians. He was quite successful at this: too successful, in fact, and his enemies had him shipped back out to the war as quickly as possible.

Vocabulary

Eumolpidae: the priests of Eleusis

flourished in his prosperity: enjoyed his successful return

Initiates, and Initiators: those involved in the religious rites

august: impressive, producing respect

venerable: producing respect, particularly because of age or wisdom

usurp: take over

People

Critias the son of Callaeschrus: Athenian political figure and author; leader of the Thirty Tyrants

On the Map

Eleusis: a town about 11 miles (18 km) from the center of Athens, which was a place of worship, particularly of the goddesses Demeter and Persephone (the *Eleusinia*).

Reading

Part One

There had been a decree for recalling Alcibiades from his banishment already passed by the people, at the instance of **Critias the son of Callaeschrus**, as appears in his elegies *[omission for length]*. But notwithstanding, the people being assembled, Alcibiades came before them, and made an oration: wherein he first lamented all his mishaps, and found himself grieved a little with the wrongs they had offered him; yet he blamed all on his cursed fortune, and some spiteful god that envied his glory and prosperity. Then he exhorted them to courage and good hope. And to conclude, the people crowned him with crowns of gold, and chose him general again of Athens, both at land and sea, with absolute power.

They also made a decree that his estate should be restored to him, and that the **Eumolpidae** and the holy herald should absolve him from the curses which they had solemnly pronounced against him by sentence of the people. Which, when all the rest obeyed, Theodorus, the high priest, excused himself. "For," said he, "if he is innocent, I never cursed him."

Part Two

Now Alcibiades **flourished in his prosperity**; yet were there some, notwithstanding, that misliked very much the time of his landing: saying it was very unlucky and unfortunate. For the day that he came into the port was the day for keeping the feast of the goddess Minerva, when all the ornaments are taken from off her image, and the part of the temple where it stands is kept close covered. Hence the Athenians esteem this day most inauspicious, and never undertake anything of importance upon it. Moreover, it was rumoured that the goddess was not content nor glad of Alcibiades' return: and that she did hide herself, because she would not see him, nor have him come near her.

Yet, notwithstanding, everything succeeded according to his wish. When the one hundred galleys that were to return (to battle) with him were fitted out and ready to sail, an honourable zeal detained him in Athens till the Celebration of the Mysteries was over. For ever since Decelea had been occupied (see **Lesson Seven**), as the enemy commanded the roads leading from Athens to **Eleusis**, the procession, being conducted by sea, had not been performed with any proper solemnity; they were forced to omit the sacrifices and dances and other holy ceremonies, which had usually been performed in the way, when they led forth Iacchus.

Alcibiades judged it would be a glorious action, which would do honour to the gods and gain him esteem with men, if he restored the ancient splendour to these rites, escorting the procession again by land, and protecting it with his army in the face of the enemy. For either, if Agis stood still and did not oppose, it would very much diminish and obscure his reputation; or, in the other alternative, Alcibiades would engage in a holy war, in the cause of the gods, and in defense of the most sacred and solemn ceremonies; and this in the sight of his country, where he should have all his fellow-citizens as witnesses of his valour.

Alcibiades being fully resolved upon this design, went and communicated it to the Eumolpidae and heralds. He placed sentinels on the tops of the hills, and at the break of day sent forth his scouts. And then taking with him the priests, **Initiates, and Initiators**, and encompassing them with his soldiers, he conducted them with great order and profound silence; an **august** and **venerable** procession; wherein all who did not envy him said he performed at once the office of a high priest and of a general. The enemy did not dare to attempt anything against them, and thus he brought them back to safety to the city.

Now this did more increase the greatness of his mind, and therewith the people's good opinion of his sufficiency, and wise conduction of an army: insomuch as they thought him invincible, having the sovereign power and authority of a general. He so won, indeed, upon the lower and meaner sort of people, that they passionately desired to have him as "tyrant" over them; and some of them did not scruple to tell him so, and to advise him to put himself out of the reach of envy by abolishing the laws and ordinances of the people, and suppressing the idle talkers that were ruining the state, that so he might act and take upon him the management of affairs, and not stand in fear of slanderous and wicked tongues.

Now, whether Alcibiades ever had any mind to **usurp** the kingdom, the matter is somewhat doubtful. But this is certain, the greatest men of the city, fearing lest indeed he meant some such thing, hastened him on shipboard as speedily as they could, appointing the colleagues whom he chose, and allowing him all other things as he desired.

Narration and Discussion

Why do you think Alcibiades chose to restore a religious procession as a way to gain favour with the Athenians? Why was it an almost foolproof plan?

Creative narration: Write or act a conversation between two Athenian souvenir sellers, or with one of their customers, on the day of the celebration.

Lesson Eleven

Introduction

Amid rumblings of discontent about the Athenian failure to magically defeat the Spartans (made even more difficult by a shortage of money and supplies), the helmsman Antiochus took them on himself at what was called the **Battle of Notium** (Plutarch does not give the name). The ensuing disaster was no surprise: the Spartans trounced the Athenian navy, and Antiochus was killed. This was only a small victory for the Spartans, but it was disastrous for Alcibiades.

Vocabulary

imputed: blamed

obols: Greek coins worth one-sixth of a drachma

constrained: forced

provocation: means of provoking the enemy to fight

scurrilous: humorously insulting; impolite

mercenary soldiers: soldiers merely hired to fight, rather than those fighting with a personal interest in the outcome

insupportable contempt: great rudeness

ostentation: showing off

long walls: walls built from a city to its port, such as from Athens to Piraeus (**Lesson Eight**).

People

Lysander: Spartan leader and admiral who brought the Peloponnesian war to an end

Cyrus: Cyrus the Younger. His father, **Darius II**, who was king of Persia from 423 B.C.-405/404 B.C., the year of Alcibiades' death, and was succeeded by Cyrus' brother **Artaxerxes II** (see **Lesson Twelve**). Cyrus was not only a prince but a general, and satrap of Lydia and Iona. He died in a battle against his brother in 401 B.C.

Antiochus: naval commander under Alcibiades; the same Antiochus who captured Alcibiades' escaped quail (**Lesson Three**)

Thrasybulus son of Thrason (#2): Alcibiades' enemy

Conon: Athenian naval commander. **Thrasyllus**, who had lost his position as commander, was reinstated after the defeat at Notium; however, **Conon** was sent to Samos in his place. The Athenians were badly defeated by the Spartans, and Conon (with the eight remaining ships) fled to Cyprus.

Historic Occasions

406 B.C.: Alcibiades exiled again after the defeat at **Notium**

405 B.C.: Battle of Aegospotami (the last major battle of the Peloponnesian War, in which the Athenian navy was destroyed)

On the Map

Andros: a Greek island, and also a town on that island

Caria (Carians): a region of western Anatolia (Asia Minor)

Thrace (Thracians): a region of southeastern Europe which includes parts of present-day Bulgaria, Greece, and Turkey

Bisanthe, Sestos: cities in Thrace (now called Tekirdağ, in present-day Turkey)

Aegospotami: a small river northeast of **Sestos**

Lampsacus: a city on the eastern side of the Hellespont

Reading

Part One

Thereupon he set sail with a fleet of one hundred ships, and, arriving at **Andros**, he there fought with and defeated the inhabitants, as well as the Lacedaemonians who assisted them. He did not, however, take the city; which gave the first occasion to his enemies for all their accusations against him. Certainly, if ever a man was ruined by his own glory, it was Alcibiades. For his continual success had produced such an idea of his courage and conduct, that if he failed in anything he undertook, it was **imputed** to his neglect, and no one would believe it was through want of power. For they thought nothing was too hard for him, if he went about it in good earnest.

They fancied, every day, that they should hear that the Isle of Chios was taken, with all the country of Ionia; they were angry they could have no news so suddenly as they wished. They never considered how extremely money was wanting, and that, having to carry on war with an enemy who had supplies of all things from a great king, he was often forced to leave his camp to seek money where he could get it, to pay his soldiers and to maintain his army.

This it was which gave occasion for the last accusation which was made against him. For **Lysander**, being sent from Lacedaemon with a commission to be admiral of their fleet, and being furnished by **Cyrus** with a great sum of money, gave every sailor four **obols** a day, whereas before they had but three. Alcibiades could hardly allow his men three obols, and therefore was **constrained** to go into **Caria** to furnish himself with money. He left the care of the fleet, in his absence, to **Antiochus**, an experienced seaman, but rash and inconsiderate, who had express orders from Alcibiades not to engage, though the enemy provoked him.

But he slighted and disregarded these direction to that degree, that, having made ready his own galley and another, he made way for Ephesus, where the enemy lay; and, as he sailed before the heads of their galleys, used every **provocation** possible, both in words and deeds. Lysander at first manned out a few ships, and pursued him. But when all the Athenian ships came in to his assistance, Lysander also brought up his whole fleet, which gained an entire victory. He slew Antiochus himself, took many men and ships, and erected a trophy.

Alcibiades, hearing this ill-favoured news, returned presently with all possible speed to Samos: and when he came thither, he went with all the rest of his fleet to offer Lysander battle. But Lysander, quietly contenting himself with his first victory, would not stir.

Part Two

Amongst others in the army who hated Alcibiades, **Thrasybulus the son of Thrason (#2)**, Alcibiades' enemy, went purposely to Athens to accuse him, and to exasperate his enemies in the city against him. Addressing the people, he represented that Alcibiades had ruined their affairs and lost their ships by mere self-conceited neglect of his duties, committing the government of the army, in his absence, to men who gained his favour by drinking and **scurrilous** talking, whilst he wandered up and down at pleasure *[omission for length and content]*. Moreover, they laid to his charge that he did fortify a castle in the country of **Thrace**, near unto the city of **Bisanthe**, for a place to retire himself unto, either because he could not, or rather that he would not, live any longer in his own country. The Athenians gave credit to this information, and showed the resentment and displeasure which they had conceived against him by choosing other generals.

As soon as Alcibiades heard of this, he immediately forsook the army, afraid of what might follow; and, collecting a body of **mercenary soldiers**, made war upon his own account against those Thracians who called themselves free, and acknowledged no king. By this means he amassed to himself a considerable treasure; and, at the same time, secured the bordering Greeks from the incursions of foreign enemies.

Part Three

Now Tydeus, Menander, and Adimanthus, the new-made generals, were at that time posted at **Aegospotami**, or "Goats' River," with all the galleys the city of Athens had left. From there they used to go out to sea every morning, and offer battle to Lysander, who lay near **Lampsacus**; and when they had done so, they would return back again, and lay all the rest of the day, carelessly and without order, in contempt of the enemy.

Alcibiades, who was not far off, did not think so slightly of their danger, nor neglect to let them know it; but, mounting his horse, came to the generals, and represented to them that they had chosen a very inconvenient station, where there was no safe harbour, and where they were distant from any town; so that they were constrained to send for their necessary provisions as far as **Sestos**; and that they suffered their mariners to leave their ships, and go a-land when they lay at anchor, straggling up and down the country without regard that there lay a great army of their enemies before them, ready to be set out at their generals' commandment: and therefore he advised them to remove thence, and to go cast anchor before the city of Sestos. But the admirals not only disregarded what he said, but Tydeus, with insulting expressions, commanded him to be gone, saying that now not he, but others, had the command of the forces.

Alcibiades, suspecting something of treachery in these words, departed, and told his friends who accompanied him out of the camp that if the generals had not used him with such **insupportable contempt**, he would within a few days have forced the Lacedaemonians, however unwilling, either to have fought the Athenians at sea or to have deserted their ships. Some looked upon this as a piece of **ostentation** only; others said that the thing was probable, for that he might have brought down by land great numbers of the Thracian cavalry and archers, to assault and disorder them in their camp.

The event, however, soon made it evident how rightly he had judged of the errors which the Athenians committed. For Lysander came so fiercely upon them on a sudden, that of all the ships they had in their whole fleet, only eight galleys were saved, with whom **Conon** fled; and the others, being not much less than two hundred in number, were every one of them taken and carried away, with three thousand prisoners whom Lysander put to death. And within a short time after, he took Athens itself, burnt all the ships which he found there, and demolished their **long walls**.

Narration and Discussion

Should Alcibiades have been blamed for the defeat at Notium, since it was due to Antiochus' disobedience?

Why did Alcibiades warn the new generals about their dangerous position? Was this magnanimous of him, or did he have other reasons?

For older students: "Certainly, if ever a man was ruined by his own glory, it was Alcibiades." Explain.

Creative narration for older students: Shakespeare often drew inspiration from Plutarch's *Lives*. Choose an event from this passage, and write or dramatize it in the style of a Shakespearean play.

Lesson Twelve and Examination Questions

Introduction

Alcibiades, fearing the Spartans, escaped to Bithynia. After being robbed, however, he decided to ask for help from the Persian satrap Pharnabazus. Meanwhile, the Spartans had taken command in Athens. The Athenians were sorry they rejected Alcibiades, and hoped he would find some way to save them again; the Spartans feared the same.

Vocabulary

despotic rulers: or despots; those who rule with absolute power

his subordinate: one below him in rank

cast away: ruined

magistrates: rulers

enterprising what was hazardous: taking a risk

mistress: female friend

asunder: apart

People

Artaxerxes: Artaxerxes II Mnemon, elder brother of Cyrus the Younger; King of Persia from about 404 BC to 358 BC

Themistocles: Athenian politician and general, hero of the Battle of Salamis during the Persian Wars, and the subject of Plutarch's *Life of Themistocles.* He died in 459 B.C., about ten years before Alcibiades was born. Like Alcibiades, he sought refuge at the court of an earlier Artaxerxes, Artaxerxes I.

Historic Occasions

404 B.C.: Official end of the Peloponnesian War

404 B.C.: Death of Alcibiades

401 B.C.: Death of Agis II

399 B.C.: Death of Socrates

395 B.C.: Assassination of Tissaphernes

On the Map

Bithynia: a region/kingdom in northwestern Asia Minor

Reading

Part One

After this, Alcibiades, standing in dread of the Lacedaemonians, who were now masters of both sea and land, retired into **Bithynia**. He sent thither great treasure before him, took much with him, but left much more in the castle where he had before resided. But he lost great part of his wealth in Bithynia, being robbed by some Thracians who lived in those parts; and thereupon he determined to go to the court of **Artaxerxes**, not doubting but that the king, if he would make trial of his abilities, would find him not inferior to **Themistocles**, besides that he was recommended by a more honourable cause. For he went not, as Themistocles did, to offer his service against his fellow-citizens, but against their enemies, and to implore the king's aid for the defense of his country. He concluded that Pharnabazus would most readily procure him a safe conduct, and therefore went into Phrygia to him, and continued to dwell there some time, paying him great respect, and being honourably treated by him.

Part Two

All this while the Athenians found themselves desolate, and in miserable state to see their empire lost: but then much more, when Lysander had taken all their liberties, and did set thirty **despotic rulers** over their city. Now too late, after all was lost (where they might have recovered again, if they had been wise) they began together to bewail and lament their miseries and wretched state, looking back upon all their willful faults and follies committed: among which, they did reckon their second time of falling out with Alcibiades was their greatest fault. For he was rejected without any fault committed by himself, and only because they were incensed against **his subordinate** for having shamefully lost a few ships, they much more shamefully deprived the commonwealth of its most valiant and accomplished general.

And yet they had some little poor hope left, that they were not altogether **cast away**, so long as Alcibiades lived, and had his health. For before, when he was a forsaken man, and led a banished life: yet he could not live idly, and do nothing. "Wherefore now much more," said they to themselves, "if there be any help at all, he will not suffer out of doubt the insolence and pride of the Lacedaemonians, nor yet abide the cruelties and outrages of these thirty tyrants."

And surely the common people had some reason to have these thoughts in their heads, considering that the thirty governors themselves did what they could possibly to spy out Alcibiades' doings, and what he went about. Insomuch as Critias represented to Lysander that the Lacedaemonians could never securely enjoy the dominion of Greece till the Athenians' democracy was absolutely destroyed; and, though now the people of Athens seemed quietly and patiently to submit to so small a number of governors, yet so long as Alcibiades lived, the knowledge of this fact would never suffer them so to be reigned over, but would attempt by all device he could to bring a change and innovation among them.

Yet Lysander would not credit these persuasions, till at last he received secret orders from the **magistrates** of Lacedaemon, expressly requiring him to get Alcibiades killed: whether it was that they feared his energy and boldness in **enterprising what was hazardous**, or else that they sought to gratify King Agis by it. Upon receipt of this order, Lysander sent away a messenger to Pharnabazus, desiring him to put it in execution. Pharnabazus committed the affair to Magaeus, his brother, and his uncle, Susamithres.

Part Three

Alcibiades resided at that time in a small village in Phrygia, together with Timandra, a **mistress** of his.

[omission for content: Alcibiades reportedly had strange dreams, including one in which Magaeus killed him]

Those that were sent to kill him dared not enter the house where he was, but set it afire round about. Alcibiades spying the fire, got such apparel and hangings as he had, and threw it on the fire, thinking to have put it out: and so casting his cloak about his left arm, took his naked sword in his other hand, and ran out of the house, himself not once touched with fire, saving his clothes were a little singed. These murderers so soon as they spied him, drew back, and stood **asunder**, and dared not one of them come near him, to stand and fight with him: but standing at a distance, they slew him with their darts and arrows.

When he was dead, the barbarians departed; and Timandra took up his dead body, and covering and wrapping it up in her own robes, she buried it as decently and as honourably as her circumstances would allow.

[omission for content]

Narration and Discussion

Plutarch says that the Athenians were correct to think of Alcibiades as a valuable ally, and the Spartans just as much so to consider him a dangerous enemy. Were they both right?

Creative narration: Write or act out a final interview with Alcibiades, in his house in Phrygia. What might his plans for the future have been?

Examination Questions

Younger Students:

1. Alcibiades "with all his great courage and quickness of understanding had many great faults and imperfections." Tell a story to illustrate a) his courage, b) his envy of Nicias.

Older Students:

1. "He esteemed these endeavours of Socrates most truly a means which the gods made use of for the care and preservation of youth…" Tell two stories to show that Alcibiades valued his relationship with Socrates.

2. (High school) "Even so, Alcibiades being puffed up with vanity…as often as Socrates took him in hand was made fast and firm by his good persuasions." Explain and illustrate.

Coriolanus

(Fifth Century B.C.)

Was Coriolanus real?

Historians such as Livy and Plutarch believed that Coriolanus was a real person who lived in the early Roman Republic. More recent scholarship has cast some doubt on his existence. Certainly it was more difficult even for a writer such as Plutarch to be clear on events several centuries removed from his own time. We will treat his *Life* in the same way as we would that of Plutarch's other subjects, although the dates of historic events will be less exact.

Versions and pronunciation of his name

In different translations, Coriolanus is called Gaius Marcius Coriolanus, or Caius Martius Coriolanus. Coriolanus was a name given to him later in life (like Publicola), so in the text he is referred to as Marcius. Since he is of the house (family) of Marcius (in Latin, the Marcii), that makes him a Marcian; with North's spelling, Martius would be a Martian. I have used Dryden's spelling; but if you are searching for information, look for the other versions as well.

Should Coriolanus have a long or short A? In Latin, you would pronounce his name **Coriolah-nus**. In English, particularly in reference to Shakespeare's play, it is often pronounced **Coriolay-nus**.

The Government of Rome

Social Classes

There were two different types of class divisions in ancient Rome. The first was family-based, between the **patricians** (the nobility) and the **plebeians** (common people), and this is one of the main points of contention in the story. The second type were property- or wealth-based classes such as the ***senatores***, the wealthiest citizens, who owned large amounts of land. The next level down, the **equestrian class** (in North's translation, the **knights of Rome**), was a "business class," made up of those who could afford horses and who made up the cavalry, or soldiers on horseback, in times of war. Besides the **equestrian** class, there were three classes of property owners; and then, lowest of all, the **proletarii**.

Were the *senatores* the same as the senators?

Often, but the two were not identical. Over the centuries, both the size of the Senate and the personal requirements for membership (age, wealth) changed. Some **plebeians** became senators along with the **patricians**.

What was an aedile, a quaestor, a consul?

The elected positions, or **magistracies**, in Rome were (starting at the bottom): quaestor, aedile, praetor, and consul. (The office of tribune was a separate position, explained below.) There were various numbers of each of these: for example, two consuls were elected each year. Ex-consuls could become censors; and a consul could become dictator if the need (usually a great emergency) arose.

Who were the tribunes?

The office of "tribune of the plebeians" or "tribune of the people" was established during the lifetime of Coriolanus (see Lesson Two). The word "tribune" was also a military term, which sometimes causes confusion; but these tribunes were elected to protect the liberties of the common people from any individual or group (such as the nobles) who might take advantage of them or suppress their rights. The position was not part of the junior-senior ranking of magistrates such as quaestor and consul; it was an office voted on by the common people (plebeians), who themselves were bound by oath to protect the tribunes from harm.

Nations Around Rome

As the story of Coriolanus belongs to an earlier time than many of Plutarch's other lives, we hear about rival tribes that were eventually conquered and became part of the Roman Republic.

Aequi or **Aequians:** An **Italic** tribe who lived to the east of Rome

Italic: Like **Latin**, this refers to the Indo-European people who spoke **Italic** languages (there were other **Italic** languages besides Latin).

Latin: The name Latin (sometimes Latian) refers to an ancient Indo-European people who moved into the Italian peninsula during the late Bronze Age (1200-900 B.C.), and lived in a region they called Latium. Starting in about 600 A.D. on, the Romans became the most powerful of the Latin tribes.

Sabines: A tribe which lived in the central Apennine Mountains. Shortly after the founding of Rome, some of the Sabines joined with the Romans and became **Latinized**. The rest fought for their independence, but eventually became part of the Roman Republic. The ancestors of Coriolanus are believed to have been Sabines.

Volsci, Volscians: The Volsci, living to the southeast, were the Romans' greatest enemies during this time. North calls them the **Volsces**. Their capital city was **Antium**, so the people living there were the **Antiates**.

Top Vocabulary Terms in Coriolanus

If you recognize the following words, you are well on your way to mastering the vocabulary of *Coriolanus*. These words will not be repeated in the vocabulary lists.

1. **check:** stop, put in check
2. **choleric:** hot-tempered. To be in **choler** is to be angry.
3. **corn:** grain, such as wheat or barley
4. **hazard:** risk
5. **sedition:** rebellion, uprisings
6. **spoil, pillage:** plunder, loot: take weapons or treasures from a defeated enemy or a captured city, or steal food from the fields of an enemy. Both words can be used as verbs (they spoiled the camp) and as nouns (they came back laden with spoils).
7. **tarry:** wait
8. **valour, valiantness:** great courage and bravery
9. **virtue:** that which is morally good or desirable
10. **voices:** votes

Shakespeare Connections

Notes on Shakespeare's play *Coriolanus* follow the discussion questions.

Coriolanus Trivia

The twentieth-century poet T.S. Eliot said that Shakespeare's *Coriolanus* was better than *Hamlet.*

Lesson One

Introduction

After a brief description of the ancestry of Gaius Marcius, we are quickly introduced to a young man who was "churlish," "choleric," "impatient," "uncivil," and "altogether unfit for any man's conversation." We may well wonder what we have gotten into! However, Plutarch also describes Marcius' "natural wit," "great heart," and fierce discipline in physical training; and our picture of Marcius becomes more complex. Where would such a combination of character qualities take someone?

Vocabulary

patrician: noble; see introductory notes

supply of water: they are credited with building aqueducts

censor: a high public office; see introductory notes

eminent: famous, respected

in their minority: when they are children

churlish: rude, mean-spirited

proof: we might say "bullet-proof"

temperance: moderation, self-control

fortitude: strength of mind that allows someone to act with courage, especially in adversity and trouble

imperious: arrogant, high-handed

stripling: youth

People

Publicola: one of the first consuls in the Roman Republic

Numa: Numa Pompilius, the legendary second king of Rome

Gaius Marcius: that is, Coriolanus; see introductory notes

Tarquinius Superbus: or Tarquin; the former king of Rome

the dictator: Aulus Postumius Albus Regillensis, general of the Roman military forces at the Battle of Lake Regillus

Historic Occasions

511 B.C.: Very approximate date of birth for Coriolanus

509 B.C.: Rome became a republic

508, 507, 504 B.C.: Publius Valerius (Publicola) was consul in Rome

503 B.C.: Death of Publicola

496 B.C.: Battle of Lake Regillus

On the Map

In this first lesson, it would be useful to look at a map of the early Roman Republic, and to locate the city of **Rome**, which was founded on the banks of the **Tiber River**.

Lake Regillus: a lake located in the remains of a volcanic crater, between Rome and the city of **Tusculum**.

Reading

Part One

The **patrician** house of the Marcii in Rome produced many men of distinction; among them was Ancus Marcius, grandson to **Numa** by his daughter, and king after Tullus Hostilius; of the same family were also Publius and Quintus Marcius, which two conveyed into the city the best and most abundant **supply of water** they have at Rome. As likewise Censorinus, who, having been twice chosen **censor** by the people, afterwards himself induced them to make a law that nobody should bear that office twice.

Gaius Marcius, whose life we intend now to write, being left an orphan by his father, and brought up under the widowhood of his mother, has shown us by experience that, although the early loss of a father may be attended with other disadvantages, yet it can hinder none from being either virtuous or **eminent** in the world, and that it is no obstacle to true goodness and excellence; however bad men may be pleased to lay the blame of their corruptions upon that misfortune and the neglect of them **in their minority**. Nor is he less an evidence to the truth of their opinion who conceive that a generous and worthy nature without proper discipline, like a rich soil without culture, is apt with its better fruits to produce also much that is bad and faulty.

For this Marcius' natural wit and great heart did marvellously stir up his courage to do and attempt notable acts. But on the other side, for lack of education, he was so choleric and impatient that he would yield to no living creature; which made him **churlish**, uncivil, and altogether unfit for any man's conversation. Those who saw with admiration how **proof** his nature was against all the softnesses of pleasure, the hardships of service, and the allurements of gain, while allowing to that universal firmness of his the respective names of **temperance**, **fortitude**, and justice, yet, in the life of the citizen and the statesman, could not choose but be disgusted at the severity and ruggedness of his deportment, and with his overbearing, haughty, and **imperious** temper. Education and study, and the favours of the Muses, confer no greater benefit on those that seek them than these humanizing and civilizing lessons, which teach our natural qualities to submitted to the limitations prescribed by reason, and to avoid the wildness of extremes.

Part Two

Those were times at Rome in which that kind of worth was most esteemed which displayed itself in military achievements; one evidence of which we find in the Latin word for virtue, which is properly equivalent to "manly courage." As if valour and all virtue had been the same thing, they used as the common term the name of the particular excellence.

But Marcius, being more inclined to the wars than any other

gentleman of his time, began from his childhood to give himself to handle weapons, and daily did exercise himself therein. And outward he esteemed armour to no purpose, unless one were naturally armed within: therefore he did so exercise his body to hardness, and all kind of activity, that he was very swift in running, strong in wrestling, and mighty in gripping, so that it was hard for any to disengage himself. Insomuch as those that would try masteries with him for strength and nimbleness, would say, when they were overcome, that all was by reason of his natural strength of body, which they said no resistance and no fatigue could exhaust.

The first time he went to the wars, being but a **stripling**, was when **Tarquinius Superbus** (that had been king of Rome, and was driven out for his pride, after many attempts made by sundry battles to come in again, wherein he was ever overcome), now entered upon this last effort, and proceeded to hazard all, as it were, upon a single throw. A great number of the Latins and other people of Italy joined their forces, and were marching with him toward the city, to procure his restoration; not, however, so much out of a desire to serve and oblige Tarquin, as to gratify their own fear and envy at the increase of the Roman greatness, which they were anxious to check and reduce. In this battle, wherein were many hot and sharp encounters of either party, Marcius valiantly fought in the sight of **the dictator**: and a Roman soldier being thrown to the ground even hard by him, Marcius straight bestrode him, and slew his assailant.

The general, after having gained the victory, crowned Marcius with a garland of oaken boughs.

[omission for length: explanation of how this crown became a Roman tradition]

Narration and Discussion

What sort of a person does Marcius seem so far? Would you want to spend time with him?

Marcius "esteemed armour to no purpose, unless one were naturally armed within." What did he mean?

Creative narration: Imagine Marcius as an action hero whose superstrength is his **fortitude**. In what situations would it be an advantage to him? When it could it be a problem?

For older students: Plutarch says that "Education and study, and the favours of the Muses, confer no greater benefit on those that seek them than these humanizing and civilizing lessons, which teach our natural qualities to submitted to the limitations prescribed by reason, and to avoid the wildness of extremes." What parts of our education most "humanize" and "civilize" us?

Shakespeare Connection

Shakespeare's plays usually jump in where the action is, so the stories of Marcius' early life are only summarized in later scenes.

Lesson Two

Introduction

Marcius, as an adult, became known for his well-defined loyalties: first to his city, as shown by his military victories; also to his mother; but finally to his social class. To him, the blurring of the lines between patricians and plebeians meant only a weakening of the noble Roman spirit, especially during a time when the young Republic needed to build itself up. However, he comforted himself and his friends with the thought that, even if they had to fight side by side with the commoners, they could at least show them who had the most "valiantness."

Vocabulary

emulation: the desire to equal or outdo others

satiate: fill up, satisfy

recompense: reward

forsake or underlive: not live up to one's previous performance

exceed and obscure: we might say "overwrite"

luster: glow, radiance

prowess: skill

laurels: leafy crowns given for athletic and military victories

felicity: happiness, good fortune

usurers: those who lend at excessively high rates of interest. Being unable to pay the **usury** means being unable to pay back the loan plus the extra amount of interest.

bondmen: indentured servants, slaves

there was, nevertheless, no moderation…: the common people, even the veterans of wars, were treated harshly by the ruling noblemen, and were given none of the protection (especially financial help) that they had been promised

lenity: lenience, easing up

redress: remedy

treat: negotiate terms, deal with

succour: assistance, aid

stood presently to their arms: took up their weapons

alacrity: cheerful readiness

embasing: lowering in power and status

People

his mother: Plutarch and Shakespeare call her Volumnia, but she is also called Veturia (see note below).

Epaminondas: a Greek general of the 4th century B.C.

took a wife: later we hear her addressed as **Virgilia** or **Vergilia.** However, the Roman historian Livy said that it was the wife of

Coriolanus who was named Volumnia, and that his mother was named Veturia.

Sabines: see introductory notes

Marcus Valerius: consul in 505 B.C.; brother of Publicola

Menenius Agrippa: Agrippa Menenius Lanatus; a former consul

Junius Brutus and **Sicinnius Vellutus:** as described here, the first "tribunes of the people"

Historic Occasions

505 B.C.: War with the Sabines

Reading

Prologue

It may be observed, in general, that when young men arrive early at fame and repute, if they are of a nature but slightly touched with **emulation**, this early attainment is apt to extinguish their thirst and **satiate** their small appetites; whereas the first distinctions of more solid and weighty characters do but stimulate and quicken them and take them away like a wind in the pursuit of honour. They look upon those marks and testimonies to their virtue not as a **recompense** received for what they have already done, but as a pledge given by themselves of what they will perform hereafter: ashamed now to **forsake or underlive** the credit they have won, or, rather, not to **exceed and obscure** all that is gone before by the **luster** of their following actions.

Part One

Marcius, having a spirit of this noble make, was ambitious always to surpass himself; and did nothing, how extraordinary soever, but he thought he was bound to outdo it at the next occasion; and, ever desiring to give continual fresh instances of his **prowess**, he added one exploit to another, and heaped up trophies upon trophies. Whereupon, the captains that came afterwards (for envy of them that went before) did contend who should most honour him, and who should bear most honorable testimony of his valiantness. Insomuch the Romans having many wars and battles in those days, Coriolanus was at them all; and there was not a battle fought from whence he returned not without **laurels** and rewards.

And whereas others made glory the end of their daring, the end of his glory was the joy he saw **his mother** did take of him. For he thought nothing made him so happy and honourable, as that his mother might hear everybody praise and commend him, that she might always see him return with a crown upon his head, and that she might still embrace him with tears running down her cheeks for joy. **Epaminondas** is similarly said to have acknowledged his feeling, that it was the greatest **felicity** of his whole life that his father and mother survived to hear of his successful generalship and his victory at Leuctra. Now as for Epaminondas, he had this good hap, to have his father and mother living, to be partakers of his joy and prosperity. But Marcius, thinking all due to his mother that had been also due to his father if he had lived, did not only content himself to rejoice and honour her, but at her desire **took a wife** also, by whom he had two children; and yet he never left his mother's house.

Part Two

Now he being grown to great credit and authority in Rome for his valiantness, it fortuned there grew sedition in the city, because the Senate did favour the rich against the common people, who did complain of the sore oppression of **usurers**, of whom they borrowed money. For those that had little were yet spoiled of that little they had by their creditors, for lack of ability to pay the **usury**: who offered their goods to be sold to them that would give most. And such as had nothing left, their bodies were laid hold of, and they were made their **bondmen**, notwithstanding all the wounds and cuts they showed, which they had received in many battles, fighting for defense of their country and commonwealth: of the which, the last war they made, was against the **Sabines**, wherein they fought upon the promise the rich men had made them, that from thenceforth they would entreat them more gently; and also upon the word of **Marcus Valerius**, chief of the Senate, who by authority of the council, and on behalf of the rich, said they should perform that which they had promised.

But after that they had faithfully served in this performance, in the last battle of all, where they overcame their enemies, **there was, nevertheless, no moderation or forbearance used**; and the senate also professed to remember nothing of that agreement, and sat without testifying the least concern to see them dragged away like slaves and their goods seized upon as formerly, there began now to be open disorders and dangerous meetings in the city. The Romans' enemies, hearing of this rebellion, did straight enter the territories of Rome with a marvellous great power, spoiling and burning all as they came.

The consuls now gave notice that all those which were of lawful age to carry weapons should come and register to go to the wars, but no man obeyed their commandment. Whereupon their chief magistrates, and many of the Senate, began to be of divided opinion among themselves. For some thought it was reasonable, they should somewhat yield to the poor people's request, and that they should a little qualify the severity of the law. Others held hard against that opinion, Marcius in particular. For he alleged that the creditors losing their money they had lent was not the worst thing that was thereby: but that the **lenity** that was favoured was a beginning of open revolt against the laws, which it would become the wisdom of the government to check at the earliest moment.

The Senate met many days in consultation about it: but in the end they concluded nothing. The poor common people seeing no **redress**, gathered themselves one day together, and one encouraging another, they all forsook the city, and encamped themselves upon a hill, called to this day "The Holy Hill," alongst the Tiber, offering no creature any hurt or violence, or making any show of actual rebellion: saving that they cried, as they went up and down, that the rich men had driven them out of the city, and that all Italy through they should find air, water, and ground to bury them in. Moreover, they said, to dwell at Rome was nothing else but to be slain, or hurt with continual wars, and fighting for defense of the rich men's goods. The Senate, being afraid of their departure, sent the most moderate and popular men of their own order to **treat** with them. **Menenius Agrippa**, their chief spokesman, after much entreaty to the people, and much plain-speaking on behalf of the Senate, concluded, at length, with this celebrated fable.

> "That on a time all the members of man's body, did rebel against the belly, complaining of it, that it only remained in the midst of the body, without doing anything, neither did bear any labour to the maintenance of the rest: whereas all other parts and members did labour painfully, and was very careful to satisfy the appetites and desires of the body. And so the belly, all this notwithstanding, laughed at their folly, and said: 'It is true, I first receive all meats that nourish man's body: but afterwards I send it again to the nourishment of other parts of the same.' Even so, (quoth he), O you, my masters and citizens of Rome: the reason is alike between the Senate and you. The counsels and plans that are there duly digested convey and secure to all of you your proper benefit and support."

A reconciliation ensued, the senate agreeing to the request of the people for the annual election of five protectors for those in need of **succour**, the same that are now called the "tribunes of the people"; and the first two they pitched upon were **Junius Brutus** and **Sicinnius Vellutus**, who had been the causers and procurers of this sedition.

Hereupon the city being grown again to good quiet and unity, the commoners **stood presently to their arms**, and followed their commanders to the war with great **alacrity**. Marcius also, though he was not a little vexed himself to see the greatness of the common people thus increased, considering it was to the **embasing** of the nobility; and also saw that other noble patricians were troubled as well as himself: he did persuade the patricians to show themselves no less forward and willing to fight for their country than the common people were; and to let them know, by their deeds and acts, that they did not so much pass the people in power and riches, as they did exceed them in true nobility and valiantness.

Narration and Discussion

If you were a Roman leader, would you have reacted differently to the protests of the common people?

Creative narration: Interview (on paper if necessary) one of the new tribunes, to get his point of view on these events in Rome.

For older students and further thought: The Christian scriptures sometimes use the metaphor of a body as well (1 Corinthians 12). Does the message given in this fable have a similar or a different viewpoint?

Shakespeare Connection

This is the opening sequence of the play. Menenius tries to avert a riot by telling "a company of mutinous Citizens" the story about the stomach. As he seems to be calming things down, Marcius enters, calls the citizens "scabs," and gives the news that the senate was creating the position of tribunes "to defend their vulgar wisdoms."

In Plutarch's story, the character of Menenius is mentioned only once, in this scene. In Shakespeare's play, he becomes a major character, a close friend and loyal supporter of Marcius.

Lesson Three

Introduction

This lesson and the one following it describe a war between the Romans and the Volsci (see the introductory notes), and particularly the siege of the city of Corioli. Because of his bravery, Marcius won the attention of the Roman general, and gained an extra name.

Vocabulary

sally: a charge out of a besieged place against the enemy

vanquished: conquered

environed: surrounded

hearken: listen

conjecturing: guessing

gallantry: bravery

compass: surround

People

Volsci: sometimes **Volscians**; a tribe which was a rival power to Rome

Cominius: Postumus Cominius Auruncus, consul in 501 and 493 B.C.

Lartius: Titus Lartius, a former consul (501 and 498 B.C.)

Cato: a Roman statesman and historian of a later time

Historic Occasions

493 B.C.: The siege of Corioli

On the Map

Corioli: also spelled Coriolis or Corioles; a town of the Volsci

Antium (Antiates): capital city of the **Volsci** (see introductory notes)

Reading

Part One

The Romans were now at war with the **Volscian** nation, whose principal city was **Corioli**. When, therefore, **Cominius** the consul had laid siege to this important place, the rest of the Volscians, fearing it would be taken, mustered up whatever force they could from all parts to relieve it, designing to give the Romans battle before the city, and so attack them on both sides. Cominius, to avoid this inconvenience, divided his army, marching himself with one body to encounter the Volscians on their approach from without, and leaving **Titus Lartius**, one of the bravest Romans of his time, to command the other and continue the siege.

Wherefore all the other Volsci fearing least that city should be taken by assault, they came from all parts of the country to save it, intending to give the Romans battle before the city, and so attack them on both sides. The consul Cominius, understanding this, divided his army also in two parts, and taking the one part with himself, he marched towards them that were drawing to the city, out of the country: and the other part of his army he left in the camp with Titus Lartius (one of the valiantest men the Romans had at that time) to resist those that would make any **sally** out of the city upon them.

So the Coriolans, making small account of them that lay in camp before the city, made a sally out upon them, in the which at the first the Coriolans had the better, and drove the Romans back again into the trenches of their camp. But Marcius being there at that time, running out of the camp with a few men with him, he slew the first enemies he met withal, and made the rest of them stay upon a sudden, crying out to the Romans that had turned their backs, and calling them again to fight with a loud voice. For he had what **Cato** thought a great point in a soldier, not only strength of hand and stroke; but also a voice and look that of themselves were a terror to an enemy.

Then there flocked about him immediately a great number of Romans: whereat the enemies were so afraid, that they soon retreated. But Marcius, not content to see them draw off and retire, did chase and follow them to their own gates that fled for life. And there, perceiving that the Romans retired back for the great number of darts and arrows which flew about their ears from the walls of the city, and that there was not one man amongst them that dared follow the fleeing enemies into the city, for that it was full of men of war, very well armed, and appointed: he did encourage his fellows with words and deeds, crying out to them that Fortune had opened the gates of the city, not so much to shelter the **vanquished** as to receive the conquerors. Seconded by a few that were willing to venture with him, he bore along through the crowd, made good his passage, and thrust himself into the gate through the midst of them, nobody at first daring to resist him.

But he, looking about him, and seeing he was entered the city with very few men to help him; and perceiving he was **environed** by his enemies that gathered round about to set upon him; did things then, as it is written, wonderful and incredible, as well for the force of his hand, as also for the agility of his body; and with a wonderful courage and valiantness, he made a lane through the midst of them, and overthrew also those he laid at. Some he made run to the furthest part of the city, and others for fear he made yield themselves, and to let fall their weapons before him; thus affording Lartius abundant opportunity to bring in the rest of the Romans with ease and safety.

Corioli being thus surprised and taken, the greater part of the soldiers employed themselves in spoiling and pillaging it, while Marcius indignantly reproached them, and exclaimed that it was a dishonourable and unworthy thing to do so, when the consul and their fellow-citizens had now perhaps encountered the other Volscians, and were hazarding their lives in battle. Howbeit, cry and say to them what he could, very few of them would **hearken** to him. Wherefore, taking those that willingly offered themselves to follow him, he went out of the city, and took his way towards that part where he understood the rest of the army was: exhorting and entreating them that followed him not to be fainthearted, and oft holding up his hands to heaven, he besought the gods to be so gracious and favourable unto him, that he might come in time to the battle, and in good hour to hazard his life in defense of his countrymen.

Part Two

It was customary with the Romans of that age, when they were moving into battle array, and were on the point of taking up their shields, and girding their coats about them, to make at the same time an unwritten will, and to name who should be their heirs, in the presence of three or four witnesses. Marcius came just while the soldiers were a-doing after that sort, and that the enemies were approached so near, as one stood in view of the other. When they saw him at his first coming, all bloody, and in a sweat, and but with a few men following him: some thereupon began to be afraid. But soon after, when they saw him run with a lively cheer to the consul and to take him by the hand, declaring how he had taken the city of Corioli, and that they saw the consul Cominius also embrace and salute him: then there was not a man but took heart again to him, and began to be of a good courage, some hearing him report, from point to point, the happy success of this exploit, and others also **conjecturing** it by seeing their gestures afar off. Then they all began to call upon the consul to march forward, and to delay no longer, but to give charge upon the enemy.

First, however, Marcius desired to know of him how the Volscians had arrayed their army, and where they had placed their best men; and the consul answered that he took the troops of the **Antiates** in the center to be their prime warriors, that would yield to none in bravery. "Let me demand and obtain of you," said Marcius, "that we may be posted against them." Cominius granted the request, with much admiration for his **gallantry**.

Then Marcius, when both armies came almost to join, advanced himself a good space before his company, and went so fiercely to give charge on those that came right against him, that they could stand no longer in his hands: he made such a lane through them, and opened a passage into the battle of the enemies. But the two wings of either side turned one to the other, to **compass** him in between them: which, the consul Cominius perceiving, he sent thither straight off the best soldiers he had about him. So the battle was marvellous bloody about Marcius, and in a very short space many were slain in the place. But in the end the Romans were so strong that they distressed the enemies, and broke their array; and scattering them, made them flee.

Then they prayed Marcius that he would retire to the camp, because they saw he was able to do no more, he was already so wearied with the great pain he had taken, and so faint with the great wounds he had upon him. But Marcius answered them that it was not for conquerors to yield, nor to be fainthearted: and thereupon he began afresh to chase those that fled, until such time as the army of the enemies was utterly overthrown, and numbers of them slain and taken prisoners.

Narration and Discussion

Tell the story of the battle at Corioli. How did Marcius show valour?

Did Marcius' concern for others surprise you?

Creative narration: Write about these events from the perspective of the Coriolans.

Shakespeare Connection

In the play, the victory at Corioli takes up most of Act I. Like Menenius, Titus Lartius is mentioned by name only once by Plutarch; but Shakespeare gives him more action and lines.

Lesson Four

Introduction

In this lesson, we see Marcius at a high point in his life: so honoured, in fact, that he is able to be magnanimous, sharing his reward with someone in much greater need.

Note: the reading has been shortened as Plutarch takes a long meander through the giving of names and nicknames, from flattering to downright insulting. Reading his examples would probably be less helpful than having an actual conversation about naming customs and the power that names/nicknames can have on one's self-concept.

Vocabulary

trappings and ornaments: an ornamental covering and other accessories

commendation: praise

mercenary: concerned only with money

contentation: contentment with what one has

abstinence: self-restraint

covetousness: wanting what one does not have

Christian name: first name

Reading

The day after, Marcius went to the consul, and the other Romans with him. There the consul Cominius, going up to his chair of state, in the presence of the whole army, gave thanks to the gods for so great, glorious, and prosperous a victory; then he spoke to Marcius, whose valiantness he commended beyond the moon, both for that which he himself saw him do with his eyes, as also for that Marcius had reported unto him. So in the end he willed that Marcius should choose out of all the horses they had taken of their enemies, and of all the goods they had won (whereof there was great store) ten of every sort which he liked best, before any distribution should be made to others. Besides this great honourable offer, he gave him a goodly horse with **trappings and ornaments**: which the whole army, beholding, did marvellously praise and commend.

But Marcius stepping forth, told the consul he most thankfully accepted the gift of his horse, and was a glad man, besides, that his service had deserved his general's **commendation**; and as for his other offer, which was rather a **mercenary** reward than an honourable recompense, he wanted none of it, but was contented to have his equal part with the other soldiers. "Only this grace," said he, "I crave, and beseech you to grant me. Among the Volsci there is an old friend and host of mine, an honest wealthy man, and now a prisoner, who living before in great wealth in his own country, liveth now a poor prisoner in the hands of his enemies: and yet notwithstanding all this his misery and misfortune, it would do me great pleasure if I could save him from this one danger: to keep him from being sold as a slave."

The soldiers hearing Marcius' words, made a marvellous great shout among them: and there were more that wondered at his great **contentation** and **abstinence**, when they saw so little **covetousness** in him, than they were that highly praised and extolled his valiantness. The very persons who conceived some envy and despite to see him so specially honoured, could not but acknowledge that one who so nobly could refuse reward was beyond others worthy to receive it; and were more charmed with that virtue which made him despise advantage, than with any of those former actions that have gained him his title to it. It is the higher accomplishment to use money well than to use arms; but not to need it is more noble than to use it *[these are Dryden's phrases;*

see North's translation below].

After this shout and noise of the assembly was somewhat appeased, the consul Cominius began to speak in this sort:

> "We cannot compel Marcius to take these gifts we offer him, if he will not receive them: but we will give him such a reward for the noble service he hath done, as he cannot refuse. Therefore we do order and decree that, henceforth, he be called Coriolanus, unless his valiant acts have won him that name before our nomination."

And so ever since, he still bore the third name of Coriolanus.

(The first name the Romans have, such as "Gaius," was our **Christian name** now. The second, such as "Marcius," was the name of their house and family. The third was some addition given, either for some act or notable service, or for some mark on their face, or of some shape of their body, or else for some special virtue they had.)

[omission for length and content]

Narration and Discussion

Why did Marcius turn down the extra rewards he was offered?

See the note about names at the beginning of the lesson. Discussion on this topic may lend itself to some form of **creative narration**.

For older students: North's translation says, "They esteemed more the virtue that was in him, that made him refuse such rewards, than that which made them to be offered him, as unto a worthy person. For it is far more commendable to use riches well than to be valiant: and yet it is better not to desire them, than to use them well." Small differences in translation can change the meaning of a passage: for instance, whether one "needs" or "desires" money. However, without splitting hairs over the words, can you explain what Plutarch meant by this?

Shakespeare Connection

Shakespeare places the scene where Marcius is offered various rewards back in Act I, right after the battle.

Lesson Five

Introduction

A rumour was started in Rome that a grain shortage had been engineered by the nobility, as a form of revenge on the common people. At the same time, the city of Velitrae was depopulated by a plague, so the government planned to send some of the "surplus Romans" in that direction and start a new colony. They also planned to send a large number of men out to fight against the Volsci, to put some of their restless energy to constructive use.

However, the tribunes wanted to know why they should send Roman citizens to live in a disease-ridden area "under a strange god"; and they were equally unsupportive of the military campaign. The people refused to participate in either plan, until Marcius stepped in.

Fueled by success, he then decided to run for consul, and expected an easy win. But the public, fickle as always, suddenly began to see him in a less friendly light.

Vocabulary

popular orators: tribunes of the people.

pretext: excuse; reason given that is not the true reason

arable: able to be farmed

provision, victuals: food supplies

corn: grain such as wheat or barley

necessity: great need due to an unfortunate situation

happy hour: good timing

meet: proper

mutinous and seditious: rebellious

the elements of disease…: the rebels were like germs causing the disease of rebellion in Rome

supply the desolation: fill the empty spaces

plausible: believable

precipitating: hurling

wanting: lacking

upon the consular summons: when the consuls called them

mustered up his own clients: hired his own soldiers

pompous: full of pomp and display

benevolence: goodwill

the proud and contentious element…: the tendency towards arrogance, unwillingness to bend to others (though he enjoyed being in a position to be generous to those of lower status), and even his hot-temperedness, all of which Marcius saw as natural to his dignity as a nobleman.

equanimity: composure and calmness in a difficult situation

ulcerations: an **ulcer** is a break on the skin or on an organ inside the body, which does not heal quickly. This image shows Marcius' anger bursting out and perhaps having similar long-term effects.

Historic Occasions

493 or 492 B.C.: The consular elections described in this passage

On the Map

Velitrae: or Velletri. An ancient city of the Volsci tribe.

Reading

Part One

The war against the Volsci was no sooner at an end than the **popular orators** revived domestic troubles, and raised another sedition, without any new cause or complaint or just grievance to proceed upon, but merely turning the very mischiefs that unavoidably ensued from their former contests into a **pretext** against the patricians. The greatest part of their **arable** land had been left unsown and unplowed, and the time of war allowing them no means or leisure to import **provision** from other countries, there was an extreme scarcity. The movers of the people then observing that there was no corn to be bought, and that if there had been they had no money to buy it, began to spread false tales and rumours against the nobility, that they, in revenge of the people, had purposely contrived the famine.

Furthermore, in the midst of this stir, there came ambassadors from **Velitrae**, that offered up their city to the Romans, and prayed them they would send new inhabitants to replenish the same: because the plague had been so extreme among them, and had killed such a number of them, as there was not left alive a tenth of the people that had been there before. So the wise men of Rome began to think that the **necessity** of Velitrae fell out in a most **happy hour**, and how by this occasion it was very **meet**, in so great a scarcity of **victuals**, to disburden Rome of a great number of citizens: and by this means as well to take away this new sedition, and utterly to rid it out of the city, as also to clear the same of many **mutinous and seditious** persons, so to say, **the elements of disease and disorder in the state**.

The consuls, therefore, singled out such citizens to **supply the desolation** at **Velitrae**; and gave notice to others that they should be ready to march against the Volsci (hoping, by the means of foreign war, to pacify their sedition at home). Moreover they imagined, when rich as well as poor, plebeians and patricians, should be mingled again the same army and the same camp, and engage in one common service for the public, it would mutually dispose them to reconciliation and friendship.

But Sicinnius and Brutus, the popular orators, interposed, crying out that the consuls disguised the most cruel and barbarous action in the world under that mild and **plausible** name of a "colony"; and were simply **precipitating** as many poor citizens into a mere pit of destruction, bidding them settle down in a country where the air was charged with disease, and the ground covered with dead bodies, and expose themselves to the evil influence of a strange and angered deity. And then, as if it would not satisfy their hatred to destroy some by hunger, and offer others to the mercy of a plague, they must proceed to involve them also in a needless war of their own making, so that no calamity might be **wanting** to complete the punishment of the citizens for refusing to submit to that of slavery to the rich.

By such addresses, the people were so possessed that none of them would appear, **upon the consular summons**, to be enlisted for the war; neither would they be sent out to this new colony: so that the Senate was at a loss what to say or do. But Marcius, who began now to bear himself higher and to feel confidence in his past actions; conscious, too, of the admiration of the best and greatest men of Rome; openly took the lead in opposing the favourers of the people. The colony was dispatched to Velitrae; those that were chosen by lot being compelled to depart upon high penalties; and when they obstinately persisted in refusing to enroll themselves for the Volscian service, he **mustered up his own clients**, and as many others as could be wrought upon by persuasion, and with these made inroad into the territories of the Antiates. There, finding a considerable quantity of corn, and collecting much booty both of cattle and prisoners, he reserved nothing for himself in private, but returned safe to Rome; while those that ventured out with him were seen laden with pillage, and driving their prey before them. This sight filled those that had stayed at home with regret for their perverseness, with envy at their fortunate fellow-citizens, and with feelings of dislike to Marcius, and hostility to his growing reputation and power, which might probably be used against the public interest.

Part Two

Shortly after this, Marcius stood for the consulship: and the common people favoured his suit, thinking it would be a shame to them to deny and refuse the chiefest nobleman of blood, and most worthy person of Rome, and especially him that had done so great service and good to the commonwealth. For the custom of Rome was, at that time, that such as did sue for any office should, for certain days before, be in the marketplace, with only a poor gown on their backs, and without any tunic underneath, to pray the citizens to remember them at the day of election: which was thus devised either to promote their supplications by the humility of their dress, or else because they might show the people their wounds they had gotten in the wars in service of the commonwealth, as manifest marks and testimony of their valiantness.)

[omission for length]

Now Marcius following this custom, showed many wounds and cuts upon his body, which he had received in seventeen years' service at the wars, and in many sundry battles, being ever the foremost man that did set out feet to fight. So that there was not a man among the people, but was ashamed of himself to refuse so valiant a man: and one of them said to another, "We must needs choose him consul, there is no remedy."

But when the day of election was come, and Marcius appeared in the Forum, with a **pompous** train of senators attending him; and the patricians all manifested greater concern, and seemed to be exerting greater efforts, than they had ever done before on the like occasion; the commons then fell off again from the kindness they had conceived for him, and in the place of their former **benevolence**, began to feel something of indignation and envy: passions assisted by the fear they entertained that if a man of such aristocratic temper, and so influential among the patricians, should be invested with the power which that office would give him, he might employ it to deprive the people of all that liberty which was yet left them. In conclusion, they rejected Marcius, and made two others consul.

The Senate was marvellously offended with the people; but Marcius took it in far worse part than the Senate, and was out of all patience. He had always indulged his temper, and had regarded **the proud and contentious element of human nature as a sort of nobleness and magnanimity**; reason and discipline had not imbued him with that solidity and **equanimity** which enters so largely into the virtues of the statesman. He had never learned how essential it is for anyone who undertakes public business, and desires to deal with mankind, to avoid above all things that self-will, which, as Plato says, belongs to the family of solitude; and to pursue, above all things, that capacity, so generally ridiculed, of submission to ill-treatment.

Marcius, straightforward and direct, and possessed with the idea that to vanquish and overbear all opposition is the true part of bravery; and never imagining that it was the weakness of his nature that broke out, so to say, in these **ulcerations** of anger, retired, full of fury and bitterness against the people.

[omission for length]

Narration and Discussion

Marcius had shown excellent leadership in the recent unrest, and he also had his share of admirable scars; why then did he lose the election for consul? What was his reaction?

Plutarch disagrees with the idea that "to vanquish and overbear all opposition is the true part of bravery." If bravery (or valour) is not solely about being strong enough to win the battle, what is its purpose? You might incorporate this discussion into a **creative narration**.

For older students: Plutarch says that potential leaders must pursue "that capacity, so generally ridiculed, of submission to ill-treatment." What does he mean? Do you agree?

Shakespeare Connection

In the play, the choice of Marcius for consul appears to flow directly out of his military victory and current popularity with the people, rather than as the separate event that Plutarch describes. The question of whether or not he will be chosen consul is drawn out until the end of Act II; and even then, in the major scene that follows (Act III. Scene i.), it's not quite clear whether Marcius knows that the tide has turned against him (Cominius addresses him as Lord Consul).

One other thing to note about Shakespeare's version is that, also in Act III. Scene i., Brutus says, "And of late, / When corn was given them gratis, you repin'd, / Scandall'd the suppliants for the people, call'd them / Time-pleasers, flatterers, foes to nobleness." In Plutarch's story, the arrival of the grain supplies, and the argument over its distribution, doesn't happen until after the consulship election is over (**Lesson Six**).

Lesson Six

Introduction

Around this time, large amounts of grain finally arrived in Rome from various sources. The first thought of the governors was that some of it should be sold cheaply, and some should be given away. Marcius violently disagreed; he said that the common people would think the grain was only given out an attempt to appease them; and that they would take advantage of that and grow even more violent, demand even more. He proposed that the experiment with the "tribuneship" be cancelled as well, since it only caused dissent. "Only a few old men" disagreed with him. It was obvious that matters in the Republic were not going well; and they were about to get much worse, especially for Marcius.

Vocabulary

deliberation: discussion

inveighed against: criticized

petulance: rudeness, insolence

***gratis*:** at no cost

rang it out: declared

break in upon the Senate: force their way into the meeting room

repulsed: shoved away

aediles: see introductory notes. One of the duties of an **aedile** was to enforce public order.

stoutness: stubbornness

wonted: customary, usual

stirred coals among the people: angered them

apprehend: arrest

Tarpeian Rock: a cliff on the southern side of the Capitoline Hill, commonly used as an execution site

tumult: confusion

beseeching the multitude: begging the crowd

what the heads of the indictment: what charges

impeached for attempting usurpation: put out of office for attempting to take over the government

designing to establish arbitrary government: as above; also translated "aspiring to be king"

mien: manner

carriage: the way he walked

countenance: face

ague: fever

even in that taking: in the state just described

Historic Occasions

491 B.C.: The conflict described in this lesson

On the Map

Syracuse: A Greek colony in Sicily

Reading

Part One

In the midst of this, a large quantity of corn reached Rome, a great part bought up in Italy, but an equal amount sent as a present from **Syracuse**, from Gelo, then reigning there. Many began now to hope well of their affairs, supposing the city, by this means, would be delivered at once both of its want and discord. A council, therefore, being presently held, the people came flocking about the senate-house, eagerly awaiting the result of the **deliberation**, expecting that the marketplaces would now be less cruel, and that what had come as a gift would be distributed as such. There were some within who so advised the Senate; but Marcius, standing up, sharply **inveighed against** those who spoke in favour of the multitude, calling them "flatterers of the rabble, traitors to the nobility"; and alleging that,

> "by such gratifications, they did but cherish those ill seeds of boldness and **petulance** that had been sown among the people, which they should have done well to observe and stifle at their first appearance, and not have suffered the plebeians to grow so strong by granting them magistrates of such authority as the tribunes. They were, indeed, even now formidable to the state since everything they desired was granted them; no constraint was put on their will; they refused obedience to the consuls and, overthrowing all law and magistracy, gave the title of magistrate to their private factious leaders. Therefore (said he), they that persuaded that the corn should be given out to the common people ***gratis***, as they used to do in cities of Greece, where the people had more absolute power, did but only nourish their disobedience, which would break out in the end, to the utter mine and overthrow of the whole state *[omission for length]*."

Marcius, dilating the matter with many such like reasons, won all the young men, and almost all the rich men to his opinion: insomuch they **rang it out** that he was the only man, and alone in the city, who stood out against the people, and never flattered them. There were only a few old men that spoke against him, fearing least some mischief might fall out upon it, as indeed there followed no great good afterward.

For the tribunes of the people, being present at this consultation of the Senate, when they saw that the opinion of Marcius was confirmed with the more voices, they left the Senate, and went down to the people, crying out for help, and that they would assemble to save their tribunes. The sum of what Marcius had spoken, having been reported to the people, excited them to such fury that they were ready to **break in upon the Senate**. The tribunes prevented this by laying all the blame on Coriolanus, whom, therefore, they cited by their messengers to come before them and defend himself. And when he contemptuously **repulsed** the officers who brought him the summons, they came themselves, with the **aediles**, proposing to carry him away by force; and, accordingly, began to lay hold on his person. The patricians, however, coming to his rescue, not only thrust off the tribunes, but also beat the aediles, that were their seconds in the quarrel; but the night approaching put an end to the contest.

Part Two

[Omission for length: the next morning, the senate agreed to send the two consuls to speak to the people, which they did. The consuls promised that the grain would be sold at a low cost, which seemed to calm most people down. Then the tribunes stood up and demanded that Marcius come and answer for the things he had said, and also that he be charged with violence against the aediles.]

All this was spoken to one of these two ends, either that Marcius, against his nature, should be constrained to humble himself, and to abase his haughty and fierce mind; or else, if he continued still in his **stoutness**, he should incur the people's displeasure and ill will so far that he should never possibly win them again. Which they hoped would rather fall out so, than otherwise: as indeed they guessed unhappily, considering Marcius' nature and disposition.

So Marcius came and presented himself to answer their accusations against him, and the people held their peace, and gave attentive ear to hear what he would say. But where they thought to have heard very humble and lowly words come from him, he began not only to use his

wonted boldness of speaking (which of itself was very rough and unpleasant, and did more aggravate his accusation, than purge his innocence) but also gave himself in his words to thunder, and look therewithal so grimly, as though he made no reckoning of the matter. This **stirred coals among the people**, who were in wonderful fury at it; and their hate and malice grew so toward him, that they could no longer bear nor endure his bravery and careless boldness.

Whereupon Sicinnius, the cruellest and stoutest of the tribunes, after he had whispered a little with his companions, did openly pronounce in the face of all the people, Marcius as condemned by the tribunes to die. He commanded the aediles to **apprehend** him, and carry him straight to the **Tarpeian Rock**, and to cast him headlong down the same. When the aediles came to lay hands upon Marcius to do that which they were commanded, divers of the people themselves thought it too cruel and violent a deed. The noblemen also being much troubled to see such force and rigour used, hurried up with cries to the rescue; and while some made actual use of their hands to hinder the arrest, and surrounding Marcius, got him in among them, others, as in so great a **tumult** no good could be done by words, stretched out theirs, **beseeching the multitude** that they would not proceed to such furious extremities.

[Omission for length: the tribunes were finally persuaded that it would be more civilized, and less dangerous, to give Marcius a proper trial. The patricians worried that if the tribunes were given full authority in the case, the common people would want even more power; others said that it would encourage a spirit of co-operation.]

Part Three

Marcius, seeing the Senate in great doubt how to resolve, partly for the love and goodwill the nobility did bear him, and partly for the fear they stood in of the people, asked aloud of the tribunes what the crimes were which they intended to charge him, and **what the heads of the indictment** they would oblige him to plead to before the people; and being told by them that he was to be **impeached for attempting usurpation**, and that they would prove him guilty of **designing to establish arbitrary government**, stepping forth upon this, "Let me go then," he said, "to clear myself from that imputation before an assembly of them; I freely offer myself to any sort of trial, nor do I refuse any kind of punishment whatsoever; only," he continued, "let what you now mention be really made my accusation, and do not you play false with the Senate." They consented to these terms.

[Omission for length: However, when Marcius came to be tried, he was accused of quite different things, including the manner in which he had distributed the spoils won at Antium. The vote went against him, and he was sentenced to perpetual (everlasting) banishment. The common people went home in triumph; the senators, in shame and confusion.]

There needed no difference of garments, I warrant you, nor outward shows, to know a plebeian from a patrician: for they were easily discerned by their looks. For he that was on the people's side, looked cheerily on the matter: but he that was sad, and hung down his head, he was surely of the noblemen's side.

Marcius alone, himself, was neither stunned nor humiliated. In **mien**, **carriage**, and **countenance**, he bore the appearance of entire composure, and, while all his friends were full of distress, seemed the only man that was not touched with his misfortune. Not that either reflection taught him, or gentleness of temper made it natural for him to submit; he was wholly possessed, on the contrary, with a profound and deep-seated fury, which passes with many for no pain at all. For when sorrow (as you would say) is set afire, then it is converted into spite and malice, and driveth away for that time all faintness of heart and natural fear. And this is the cause why the choleric man is so altered, and mad in his actions, as a man set afire with a burning **ague**: for when a man's heart is troubled within, his pulse will beat marvellous strongly. Now that Marcius was **even in that taking**, it appeared true soon after by his doings.

For when he was come home to his house again, and had taken his leave of his mother and wife, finding them weeping, and shrieking out for sorrow, and had also comforted and persuaded them to be content with his chance: he went immediately to the gate of the city, accompanied with a great number of patricians that brought him thither, from whence he went on his way with three or four of his friends only, taking nothing with him, nor requesting anything of any man.

Narration and Discussion

Marcius made a deal with the tribunes that he would only answer to one charge, that of attempting to take over the government. What happened at his trial?

How does Plutarch explain Marcius' apparent lack of emotion after his banishment?

Creative narration #1: Plutarch says that after the events described, the common people went home "cheerily," but the nobility, in shame and grief. Create a conversation or diary entry from the viewpoint of the observers.

Creative narration #2: You are a reporter who has been given an exclusive interview with Marcius. What questions will you ask him?

Shakespeare Connection

In Act III. Scene i., Coriolanus says, in front of the tribunes, "Let what is meet be said it must be meet, / And throw their power i' th' dust." Officers are called in to arrest him, and, after a scuffle, the tribunes propose that he be thrown from the Tarpeian Rock; but eventually they agree to a trial by law. Act III ends with Marcius' banishment; Act IV opens with his farewell to his family.

Lesson Seven

Introduction

Marcius, after the initial shock of his banishment, began to think of a way to get revenge on Rome.

Vocabulary

striving in all emulation of honour: trying to be the most admired

the common quarrel between them: the Roman-Volsci enmity

horde: group, crowd

for my surname of Coriolanus: Marcius earned his name because of his victory over the Volsci.

sufferance: tolerance (in this case, of injustice)

dastardly: wicked, evil

that thou dare not: if you will not trust me to help you, and will therefore have me put to death

proffering: offering, holding something out

palsy: paralysis, especially accompanied by tremors

litter: stretcher, movable bed

People

Tullus Aufidius: Commander of the Volscian army; enemy of Marcius.

Reading

Prologue

Marcius continued solitary for a few days in a place in the country, distracted with a variety of counsels, such as rage and indignation, suggested to him; proposing to himself no honourable or useful end, but only that he might best satisfy his revenge on the Romans, he resolved at length to raise up a heavy war against them from their nearest neighbours.

He determined first to make trial of the Volsci, whom he knew to be still vigorous and flourishing, both in men and treasure; and he imagined their force and power was not so much abated, as their spite and anger increased, by the recent overthrows they had received from the Romans.

Part One

Now in the city of Antium, there was one called **Tullus Aufidius**, who for his riches, as also for his nobility and valiantness, was honoured among the Volsci as a king. Marcius knew very well that Tullus did more malice and envy him than he did all the Romans besides; because that many times in battles where they met, they were ever at the encounter one against another, like lusty courageous youths, **striving in all emulation of honour**. Insomuch, as besides **the common quarrel between them**, there was bred a marvellous private hate one against another. Yet notwithstanding *[omission for length]*, he disguised himself in such array and attire as he thought no man could ever have known him for the person he was, seeing him in that apparel he had upon his back; and as Homer said of Ulysses,

> So did he enter into the enemies' town.

It was even twilight when he entered the city of Antium, and many people met him in the streets, but no man knew him. So he went directly to Tullus Aufidius' house, and when he came thither, he got him up straight to the chimney of the hearth, and sat him down, and spoke not a word to any man, his face all muffled over. They of the house spying him, wondered what he should be, and yet they dared not bid him rise. For ill-favouredly muffled and disguised as he was, yet there appeared a certain majesty in his countenance, and in his silence; whereupon they went to Tullus, who was at supper, to tell him of the strange disguising of this man. Tullus rose presently from the **horde**, and coming towards him, asked him what he was, and wherefore he came. Then Marcius unmuffled himself, and after he had paused a while, making no answer, he said unto him:

> "If thou knowest me not yet, Tullus, and seeing me, dost not perhaps believe me to be the man I am indeed, I must of necessity bewray myself to be that which I am. I am Gaius Marcius, who hath done to thyself particularly, and to all the Volsci generally, great hurt and mischief, which I cannot deny **for my surname of Coriolanus** that I bear. For I never had other benefit, nor recompense, of all the true and painful service I have done, and the

> extreme dangers I have been in, but only this surname: a good memory and witness of the malice and displeasure thou shouldst bear me. Indeed, the name only remaineth with me: for the rest, the envy and cruelty of the people of Rome have taken from me, by the **sufferance** of the **dastardly** nobility and magistrates, who have forsaken me, and let me be banished by the people. This extremity hath now driven me to come as a poor suitor, to take thy chimney hearth, not of any hope I have to save my life thereby. For if I had feared death, I would not have come hither to have put my life in hazard: but pricked forward with spite and desire, I have to be revenged of them that thus have banished me, whom now I begin to be avenged on, putting my person between thy enemies. Wherefore, if thou hast any heart to be wrecked of the injuries thy enemies have done thee, speed thee now, and let my misery serve thy turn, and so use it, as my service may be a benefit to the Volsci: promising thee, that I will fight with better goodwill for all you, than ever I did when I was against you, knowing that they fight more valiantly, who know the force of their enemy, than such as have never proved it. And if it be so **that thou dare not**, and that thou art weary to prove Fortune anymore: then am I also weary to live any longer. And it were no wisdom in thee, to save the life of him who hath been heretofore thy mortal enemy, and whose service now can nothing help nor pleasure thee."

Tullus, hearing what he said, was a marvellous glad man, and taking him by the hand, he said unto him: "Stand up, O Marcius, and be of good cheer, for in **proffering** thyself unto us, thou doest us great honour; and by this means thou mayest hope also of greater things at all the Volscian hands."

So he feasted him for that time, and entertained him in the honourablest manner he could, talking with him in no other matters at that present: but within a few days after, they fell to consultation together, in what sort they should begin their wars.

Part Two

Now on the other side, the city of Rome was in marvellous uproar and discord, the nobility against the commonalty, and chiefly for Marcius' condemnation and banishment. Moreover the priests, the soothsayers, and private men also, came and declared to the Senate certain sights and wonders in the air, which they had seen, and were to be considered of: amongst the which, such a vision happened. There was a citizen of Rome called Titus Latinus, a man of mean quality and condition, but otherwise an honest sober man, given to a quiet life, without superstition, and much less to vanity or lying. This man had a vision in his dream, in the which he thought that Jupiter appeared unto him, and commanded him to signify to the Senate that they had caused a bad and unacceptable dancer to go before a procession. Having beheld the vision, he said, he did not much attend to it at the first appearance; but after he had seen it a second and third time, he had lost a son, and was himself struck with a **palsy**. He was brought into the senate on a **litter** to tell this, and the story goes that he had no sooner delivered his message there, but he at once felt his strength return and got upon his legs, and went home alone without need of any support.

[Omission for length: The dreams of Titus Latinus, and the efforts of the Romans to placate the gods with a new procession, do not seem to have directly involved Martius; but they illustrate the belief that the banishment of Martius had also displeased those gods.]

Narration and Discussion

Do you think Marcius will fully give himself to the Volscian cause, or should Tullus perhaps be cautious about trusting him? What about the other way around: can Marcius trust the Volscians?

For older students and further thought: Richard Brookhiser, writing about Benedict Arnold (*Claremont Review of Books*, Winter 2019), said that one thing that set Arnold apart from those who did not defect was that his honour, though genuine, "seems to have been fatally self-contained." In other words, he recognized no purpose other than what he himself decided was important. If Coriolanus lived by the same beliefs, did that make him a hero, or was it a flaw in his character?

Creative narration: This scene lends itself to dramatization. If you are working with a group, act out the conversation between Marcius and Tullus; then read or watch Shakespeare's version.

Shakespeare Connection

These events are dramatized in Act IV, Scenes iv. and v. (Did you know that Shakespeare uses the word "thwack?")

Lesson Eight

Introduction

Marcius, as agreed, began to use his military skills on behalf of the Volsci; and they, on their side, started to value him as a gifted leader and "their only captain." But being too good at a job can sometimes become a problem.

Vocabulary

dissension: conflict, disagreement

embracing: accepting

they had sworn to a truce...: they had made a peace treaty

spectacles: the athletic games and other events relating to the holiday

nettled: annoyed

tract of time: delay

munition and furniture: military equipment, weapons

malice: desire to harm

stir and broil: disturbance, tumult

in garrison: in the fort; acting as defense

provide all conveniences…: send weapons, armour, and food to the part of the army that was fighting away from home

On the Map

Lavici: a town near modern-day Colonna

Bola: or Bolae. An ancient city believed to be on the same site as present-day Labico, a municipality within the Metropolitan City of Rome

Reading

Part One

Now Tullus and Marcius conferred secretly with the greatest personages of the city of Antium, declaring unto them that now they had good time offered them to make war with the Romans, while they were in **dissension** one with another. And when shame appeared to hinder them from **embracing** the motion, as **they had sworn to a truce and cessation of arms** for the space of two years, the Romans themselves soon furnished them with a pretense. For on a holy day, they made a proclamation, out of some jealousy or slanderous report, in the midst of the **spectacles**, that all the Volscians who had come to see them should depart the city before sunset. Some affirm that this was a contrivance of Marcius, who sent a man privately to the consuls, falsely to accuse the Volscians of intending to fall upon the Romans during the games, and to set the city on fire.

This open proclamation made all the Volsci more offended with the Romans than ever they were before; and Tullus, aggravating the matter, did so inflame the Volsci against them, that in the end they sent their ambassadors to Rome, to summon them to deliver their lands and towns again which they had taken from them in times past, or to look for present wars.

The Romans hearing this, were marvellously **nettled**: and made no other answer but thus: "If the Volsci be the first that begin war, the Romans will be the last that will end it." Immediately upon the return of the Volsci ambassadors, and the delivery of the Romans' answer, Tullus caused an assembly general to be made of the Volsci, and concluded to make war upon the Romans. This done, Tullus did counsel them to take Marcius into their service, and not to mistrust him for the remembrance of anything past, but boldly to trust him in any matter to come: for he would do them more service in fighting for them than ever he did them displeasure in fighting against them.

So Marcius was called forth, who spoke so excellently in the presence of them all, that he was thought no less eloquent in tongue than warlike in show: and declared himself both expert in wars, and wise with valiantness. Thus he was joined in commission with Tullus as general of the Volsci, having absolute authority between them to follow and pursue the wars.

But Marcius, fearing lest **tract of time** to bring this army together, with all the **munition and furniture** of the Volsci, would rob him of the means he had to execute his purpose and intent, left orders with the rulers and chief of the city to assemble the rest of their power, and to prepare all necessary provision for the camp. Then he, with the lightest soldiers he had, and those that were willing to follow him, stole away upon the sudden, and marched with all speed, and entered the territories of Rome before the Romans heard any news of his coming. Insomuch the Volsci found such spoil in the fields, as they had more than they could spend in their camp, and were weary to drive and carry away that they had. Howbeit, the gain of the spoil and the hurt they did to the Romans in this invasion was the least part of his intent.

For his chiefest purpose was to increase still the **malice** and dissension between the nobility and the commonalty: and to draw that on, he was very careful to keep the noblemen's lands and goods safe from harm and burning, but spoiled all the whole country besides, and would suffer no man to take or hurt anything of the noblemen's. This made greater **stir and broil** between the nobility and people than there was before. For the noblemen fell out with the people, because they had so unjustly banished a man of so great valour and power. The people, on the other side, accused the nobility, how they had procured Marcius to make these wars to be revenged of them: because it pleased them (the nobility) to see their goods burnt and spoiled before their eyes, whilst they themselves were well at ease, and did behold the common people's losses and misfortunes, and knowing their own goods safe and out of danger, and how the war was not made against the noblemen, that had the enemy abroad, to keep that which they had in safety.

Part Two

Now Marcius, having done this first exploit (which made the Volsci bolder, and less fearful of the Romans), brought home all the army again, without loss of any man.But when the whole strength of the Volsci was brought together in the field, with great expedition and alacrity, it appeared so considerable a body that they agreed to leave part **in garrison**, for the security of their towns; and with the other part to march against the Romans. So Marcius bade Tullus choose, and take which of the two charges he liked best. Tullus answered that he knew by experience that Marcius was no less valiant than himself, and how he ever had better fortune and good hap in all battles, than he himself had. Therefore he thought it best for him to have the leading of those that should make the wars abroad: and he himself would keep home, to provide for the safety of the cities and of his country, and to **provide all conveniences for the army abroad**.

So Marcius, being stronger than before, went first of all unto Circaeum, a Roman colony, who willingly yielded themselves, and therefore had no hurt. From thence, he entered and laid waste the country of the Latins, where he expected the Romans would meet him, as the Latins were their confederates and allies, and had often sent to demand aid from them. The people, however, on their part, showing little inclination for the service, and the consuls themselves being unwilling to run the hazard of a battle when the time of their office was almost ready to expire, they dismissed the Latin ambassadors without any effect; so that Marcius, finding no army to oppose him, marched up to their cities; and having taken by force Toleria, **Lavici**, Peda, and **Bola**, all of which offered resistance, he not only plundered their houses, but made a prey likewise of their persons. Meantime he showed particular regard for all such as came over to his party, and, for fear they might sustain any damage against his will, he removed his camp as far from their confines as he could.

When he took the city of Bola by assault, he had a marvellous great spoil; and put every man to the sword that was able to carry weapons.

The other Volsci that were appointed to remain in garrison for defense of their country, bearing this good news, would tarry no longer at home, but armed themselves, and ran to Marcius' camp, saying they did acknowledge no other captain but him. Hereupon his fame ran through all Italy, and universal wonder prevailed at the sudden and mighty revolution in the fortunes of two nations which the loss and the accession of a single man had effected.

Narration and Discussion

What was Marcius' real goal, according to Plutarch?

What were the strategies that Marcius and Tullus used against the cities under Roman rule? Why did the Romans not offer a better defense?

Creative narration: "Universal wonder prevailed at the sudden and mighty revolution in the fortunes of two nations...." As the editor, reporter, and political cartoonist of the Rome Daily News, how would you express this to your readers?

Shakespeare Connection

Shakespeare writes this section from an unexpected point of view: the Romans, including Menenius and the tribunes, receiving the news that the Volscians are camped in their territory and planning to attack. "And who's that with them?" "Can't be . . ."

Lesson Nine

Introduction

As Marcius continued on the warpath against Rome, the belief that he should be called home again was spreading; however, the senators were reluctant to act. When he camped right outside their gates, they finally agreed to send some envoys to discuss matters with him. Perhaps now that he had shown everyone what he could do, he would be happy to be welcomed home.However, the Roman ambassadors found that the new "General of the Volsci" was not so easily appeased.

Vocabulary

averse from...: refusing to do something

humour: stubborn desire

condole: sympathize

strait: tight situation

appeased: soothed, calmed

kinsman: relative; one of the same tribe

respite: period of rest

People

Aeneas: the legendary founder of Rome

On the Map

Lavinium: A port city that was considered sacred by the Romans.

Reading

Part One

All at Rome was in great disorder: they were utterly **averse from** fighting, and spent their whole time in schemes, disputes and reproaches against each other; until news was brought that the enemy had laid close siege to **Lavinium**, in which were all the temples and images of the gods their protectors, for they believed that **Aeneas** at his first arrival into Italy did build that city.

Then fell there out a marvellous sudden change of mind among the common people, and far more strange and contrary in the nobility. For the people thought good to repeal the condemnation and exile of

Marcius; whereas the Senate, being assembled to consider the decree, opposed and finally rejected the proposal, either out of the mere **humour** of contradicting and withstanding the people in whatever they should desire; or because they were unwilling, perhaps, that he (Marcius) should owe his restoration to their kindness; or having now conceived a displeasure against Marcius himself, who was bringing distress upon all alike, though he had not been ill-treated by all, and was become a declared enemy to his whole country, though he knew well enough that the principal and all the "better" men **condoled** with him, and suffered in his injuries. Report being made of the Senate's resolution, the people found themselves in a **strait**: for they could authorize and confirm nothing by their voices, unless it had been first propounded and ordained by the Senate.

But Marcius hearing this stir about him, was in a greater rage with them than before: insomuch as he raised his siege immediately before the city of Lavinium, and, going towards Rome, lodged his camp at the Cluilian ditches, about five miles from the city. His encamping so near Rome did put all the whole city in a wonderful fear: howbeit for the present time it **appeased** the sedition and dissension betwixt the nobility and the people. For there was no consul, senator, nor magistrate, that dared once contrary the opinion of the people for the calling home again of Marcius. When they saw the women in a marvellous fear, running up and down the city; the temples of the gods full of old people, weeping bitterly in their prayers to the gods; and finally, not a man either wise or hardy to provide for their safety: then they were all of opinion that the people had reason to call home Marcius again, to reconcile themselves to him, and that the Senate, on the contrary part, were in marvellous great fault to be angry with him, when it stood them upon rather to have gone out and entreated him. So they all agreed together to send ambassadors unto him, to let him understand how his countrymen did call him home again, and restored him to all his goods, and besought him to deliver them from this war.

Part Two

The ambassadors that were sent were Marcius' familiar friends and acquaintance, who looked at the least for a courteous welcome of him, as of their familiar friend and **kinsman**. Howbeit they found nothing less. For at their coming, they were brought through the camp, to the place where he was set in his chair of state with a marvellous and an unspeakable majesty, having the chiefest men of the Volsci about him: so he commanded them to declare openly the cause of their coming. Which they delivered in the most humble and lowly words they possibly could devise, and with all modest countenance and behaviour agreeable for the same.

When they had done their message: for the injury they had done him, he answered them very hotly, and in great choler. But as general of the Volsci, he willed them to restore unto the Volsci all their lands and cities they had taken from them in former wars: and moreover, that they should give them the like honour and freedom of Rome, as they had before given to the Latins. For otherwise they had no other means to end this war, if they did not grant these honest and just conditions of peace. Thereupon he gave them thirty days' **respite** to make him answer.

Narration and Discussion

Why were the Romans in a "strait" as to what to do about Marcius?

Why did Marcius' arrival near Rome actually ease some of the tension between the nobility and the common people?

Creative narration: You are one of the ambassadors sent to plead with Marcius to end the war and come back to Rome. Consider what you might say to persuade him.

For further thought: In the Book of Genesis, Joseph is approached by his brothers who have come to beg for food; but he acts the part of a stern Egyptian ruler and does not immediately disclose his true identity. Would you guess that Coriolanus is also stretching out the scene, and planning to give in when it suits him; or does he have no intention of returning?

Shakespeare Connection

The play proceeds pretty much in order from this point on, although

Shakespeare does make a few changes. It's clear, in the play, that Aufidius plans to get rid of Marcius, and that all his co-operation has been only for his own purposes.

Lesson Ten

Introduction

The back-and-forth continued between Marcius and various envoys from Rome. He was determined not to back down until the Volscian cities were restored and their other demands were granted; but he seemed to have to continually prove his fitness for that position, as even a small retreat (during the short truce with Rome itself, though not with its allies) brought his loyalties into question.

Vocabulary

blemished: damaged, dirtied

malcontents: those who were not happy with the situation

loath: reluctant

safe conduit: safe passage through the Volscian lines.

repulse: repel, push back

ill-boding: ominous, bad-sounding

Reading

Part One

So the ambassadors returned straight to Rome, and Marcius forthwith departed with his army out of the territories of the Romans. This was the first matter wherewith the Volsci (those that most envied Marcius' glory and authority) did charge Marcius with. Among those, Tullus was chief: who though he had received no private injury or displeasure of

Marcius, yet the common fault and imperfection of man's nature wrought in him; and it grieved him to see his own reputation **blemished** through Marcius' great fame and honour, and so himself to be less esteemed of the Volsci than he was before. This fell out the more because every man honoured Marcius, and thought he only could do all, and that all other governors and captains should be content with that share of power which he might think fit to accord.

From hence the first seeds of complaint and accusation were scattered about in secret, and the **malcontents** met and heightened each other's indignation, saying that to retreat as he did was in effect to betray and deliver up, though not their cities and their arms, yet what was as bad, the critical times and opportunities for action, on which depend the preservation or the loss of everything else; since in less than thirty days' space, for which he had given a respite for the war, there might happen the greatest changes in the world. Yet Marcius spent not any part of the time idly, but attacked the confederates of the enemy, ravaged their land, and took from them seven great and populous cities in that interval. The Romans dared not once put themselves into the field to come to their aid and help: they were so fainthearted, so mistrustful, and **loath** besides to make wars *[omission for length]*.

Part Two

Wherefore, the time of peace expired, and Marcius being returned into the dominions of the Romans again with all his army: they sent another embassy unto him, to pray peace and the remove of the Volsci out of their country, that afterwards they might with better leisure fall to such agreements together as should be thought most meet and necessary. For the Romans were no men that would ever yield for fear. But if he thought the Volsci had any ground to demand reasonable articles and conditions, all that they would reasonably ask should be granted unto by the Romans, who of themselves would willingly yield to reason, conditionally that they did lay down arms.

Marcius, to that, answered that, as general of the Volsci, he would reply nothing unto it. But yet as a Roman citizen, he would counsel them to let fall their pride, and to be conformable to reason, if they were wise: and that they should return again within three days, delivering up the articles agreed upon, which he had first delivered them. Or otherwise, that he would no more give them assurance or **safe conduit** to return again into his camp, with such vain and frivolous messages.

Part Three

When the ambassadors were returned to Rome, and had reported Marcius' answer to the Senate: their city being in extreme danger, and as it were in a terrible storm or tempest, they threw out (as the common proverb sayeth) their holy anchor. For then they appointed all the priests, keepers of holy things, and soothsayers to go to Marcius, appareled as when they do their sacrifices: first to entreat him to leave off war, and then that he would speak to his countrymen, and conclude peace with the Volsci.

Marcius suffered them to come into his camp, but yet he granted them nothing the more, neither did he entertain them or speak more courteously to them than he did the first time that they came unto him, saving only that he willed them to take the one of the two: either to accept peace under the first conditions offered, or else to receive war. When this solemn application proved ineffectual, the priests, too, returning unsuccessful, they determined to sit still within the city and keep watch about their walls, intending only to **repulse** the enemy, should he offer to attack them; and placing their hopes chiefly in time and in extraordinary accidents of fortune. As to themselves, they felt incapable of doing anything for their own deliverance; mere confusion and terror and **ill-boding** reports possessed the whole city.

[omission for length]

Narration and Discussion

Why did Marcius refuse to explain why the Volsci believed they had a reasonable right to the captured cities? Why did he then give them a second reply "as a Roman citizen?"

Creative narration: "...mere confusion and terror and ill-boding reports possessed the whole city." You are again the entire staff of the Rome Daily News. What will the headlines be? Will there be an advice column, or a cartoon?

Shakespeare Connection

Plutarch speaks generally of "ambassadors" that were sent to try to talk Marcius into retreating; Shakespeare makes more deliberate use of the characters, moving from the lowest personal involvement (Cominius) through close friendship (Menenius) and then finally the scene with his mother and wife (described in **Lesson Eleven**).

Lesson Eleven

Introduction

Marcius had a close relationship with his family, especially his mother. Yet it was not the rulers who thought of asking her to go and offer a final plea to her son, but another woman who had spent a lifetime observing Roman politics: Valeria, the sister of Publicola.

Vocabulary

suppliants: those who pray or worship

expedient: way to solve a problem; means of attaining an end

clemency: mercy, forgiveness

rancour: anger

raiment: clothing

amity: friendship

to be chronicled: to be put into the history books

People

Publicola: see notes for **Lesson One**

Reading

Part One

In the perplexity which I have described, the Roman women went, some to other temples, but the greater part, and the ladies of highest rank, to the altar of Jupiter Capitolinus. Among these **suppliants** was Valeria, sister to the great **Publicola**, who did the Romans eminent service both in peace and war. Publicola himself was now deceased, as is told in his *Life*; but Valeria lived still, and enjoyed great respect and honour at Rome. She, happily lighting, not without divine guidance, on the right **expedient**, both rose herself, and bade the others rise, and went directly with them to the house of Volumnia, the mother of Marcius. And coming into her, they found her, and Marcius' wife, her daughter-in-law set together, and having her young children in her lap.

Now all the train of these ladies sitting in a ring round about her: Valeria first began to speak in this sort unto her:

> "We that now make our appearance, O Volumnia, and you, Vergilia, are come as mere women to women, not by direction from the Senate, nor commandment of other magistrate: but through the inspiration (as I take it) of some god above. Who, having taken compassion and pity of our prayers, hath moved us to come unto you, to entreat you in a matter as well beneficial for us, as also for the whole citizens in general: but to yourselves in especial (if it please you to credit me) and shall redound to our more fame and glory, than the daughters of the Sabines obtained in former age, when they procured loving peace, instead of hateful war, between their fathers and their husbands. Come on, good ladies, and let us go all together unto Marcius, to entreat him to take pity upon us, and also to report the truth unto him, how much you are bound unto the citizens: who notwithstanding they have sustained great hurt and losses by him, yet they have not hitherto sought revenge upon your persons by any discourteous usage, neither ever conceived any such

thought or intent against you, but do deliver ye safe into his hands, though thereby they look for no better grace or **clemency** from him."

When Valeria had spoken this unto them, all the other ladies together with one voice confirmed that which she had said. Then Volumnia in this sort did answer her:

"My good ladies, we are partakers with you of the common misery and calamity of our country, and yet our grief exceedeth yours the more, by reason of our particular misfortune: to feel the loss of my son Marcius' former valiancy and glory, and to see his person environed now with our enemies in arms, rather to see him forthcoming and safe kept, than of any love to defend his person. But yet the greatest grief of our heaped mishaps is to see our poor country brought to such extremity, that all hope of the safety and preservation thereof is now unfortunately cast upon us simple women: because we know not what account he will make of us, since he hath cast from him all care of his natural country and commonweal, which heretofore he has held more dear and precious than either his mother, wife, or children. Notwithstanding, if ye think we can do good, we will willingly do what you will have us: bring us to him I pray you. For if we cannot prevail, we may yet die at his feet as humble suitors for the safety of our country."

Her answer ended, she took her daughter-in-law, and Marcius' children with her, and being accompanied with all the other Roman ladies, they went in **troop** together unto the Volsci camp: whom when they saw, they of themselves did both pity and reverence her, and there was not a man among them that once dared say a word unto her.

Part Two

Now was Marcius set then in his chair of state, with all the honours of a general; and when he had spied the women coming afar off, he marvelled what the matter meant: but afterwards recognizing his wife, who came foremost, he determined at the first to persist in his obstinate and inflexible **rancour**. But overcome in the end with natural affection, and being altogether altered to see them, his heart would not serve him to tarry their coming to his chair; but coming down in haste, he went to meet them, and first he kissed his mother, and embraced her a pretty while, than his wife and little children. And nature so wrought with him that the tears fell from his eyes, and he could not keep himself from making much of them, but yielded to the affection of his blood, as if he had been violently carried with the fury of a most swift running stream.

After he had thus lovingly received them, and perceiving that his mother Volumnia would begin to speak to him, he called the chiefest of the council of the Volsci to hear what she would say. Then she spoke in this sort:

> "If we held our peace (my son) and determined not to speak, the state of our poor bodies, and present sight of our **raiment**, would easily bewray to thee what life we have led at home, since thy exile and abode abroad.
>
> "But think now with thyself, how much more unfortunately, than all the women living we are come hither, considering that the sight which should be most pleasant to all other to behold, spiteful fortune hath made most fearful to us: making myself to see my son, and my daughter here, her husband, besieging the walls of his native country. So as that which is the only comfort to all other in their adversity and misery, to pray unto the gods, and to call to them for aid: is the only thing which plunges us into most deep perplexity. For we cannot (alas) together pray, both for victory, for our country, and for safety of thy life also: but a world of grievous curses, yea more than any mortal enemy can heap upon us, are forcibly wrapped up in our prayers. For the bitter sop of most hard choice is offered thy wife and children, to forego the one of the two: either to lose the person of thyself, or the nurse of their native country *[omission for length]*.

> "For as to destroy thy natural country, it is altogether unmeet and unlawful: so were it not just, and less honorable, to betray those that put their trust in thee. But my only demand consisteth, to make equal delivery of all evils, which delivereth equal benefit and safety, both to the one and the other, but most honorable for the Volsci. For it shall appear, that having victory in their hands, they have of special favour granted us singular graces: peace, and **amity**, albeit themselves have no less part of both than we. Of which good, if so it came to pass, thyself is the only author, and so hast thou the only honour. But if it fail, and fall out contrary: thyself alone deservedly shall carry the shameful reproach and burden of either party. So, though the end of war be uncertain, yet this notwithstanding is most certain: that if it be thy chance to conquer, this benefit shalt thou reap of thy goodly conquest, **to be chronicled** the plague and destroyer of thy country. And if fortune also overthrow thee, then the world will say that through desire to revenge thy private injuries, thou hast forever undone thy good friends, who did most lovingly and courteously receive thee."

Marcius gave good ear unto his mother's words, without interrupting her speech at all: and after she had said what she would, he held his peace a pretty while, and answered not a word. Hereupon she began again to speak unto him, and said:

> "My son, why dost thou not answer me? Dost thou think it good altogether to give place unto thy choler and desire of revenge, and thinkest thou it not honesty for thee to grant thy mothers request, in so weighty a cause? Dost thou take it honourable for a nobleman to remember the wrongs and injuries done him: and dost not in like case think it an honest nobleman's part, to be thankful for the goodness that parents do show to their children, acknowledging the duty and reverence they ought to bear unto them? No man living is more bound to

> show himself thankful in all parts and respects, than thyself: who so unnaturally showeth all ingratitude. Moreover, my son, thou hast sorely taken of thy country, exacting grievous payments upon them in revenge of the injuries offered thee: besides, thou hast not hitherto showed thy poor mother any courtesy. And therefore, it is not only honest, but due unto me, that without compulsion I should obtain my so just and reasonable request of thee. But since by reason I cannot persuade thee to it, to what purpose do I defer my last hope?"

And with these words, herself, his wife and children, fell down upon their knees before him. Marcius seeing that, could refrain no longer, but went straight and lifted her up, crying out: "Oh mother, what have you done to me?" And holding her hard by the right hand, "Oh mother," said he, "you have won a happy victory for your country, but mortal and unhappy for your son: for I see myself vanquished by you alone." These words being spoken openly, he spoke a little apart with his mother and wife, and then let them return again to Rome, for so they did request him.

Narration and Discussion

What is it that Volumnia and the other women wanted Marcius to do?

"Oh mother," said he, "you have won a happy victory for your country, but mortal and unhappy for your son: for I see myself vanquished by you alone." What did Marcius mean?

Creative narration: This scene lends itself easily to dramatization, art, and other creative expression.

Shakespeare Connection

Shakespeare gives us a conversation (Act V Scene iv.) between Menenius and Sicinnius (spelled Sicinius Velutus), where they wonder if Marcius will listen to his mother's pleas. It includes these lines:

Sicinius Velutus: Is't possible that so short a time can alter the condition of a man!

Menenius Agrippa: There is differency between a grub and a butterfly; yet your butterfly was a grub. This Coriolanus is grown from man to dragon: he has wings; he's more than a creeping thing.

Sicinius Velutus. He loved his mother dearly.

Menenius Agrippa. So did he me: and he no more remembers his mother now than an eight-year-old horse.

Lesson Twelve and Examination Questions

Introduction

Plutarch says that the Volscian soldiers followed Marcius' command to retreat, but more from respect for his virtue than from fear of his authority. Even with amount of that support behind him, he seemed to fear what might happen when they arrived back at Antium.

Vocabulary

unfavourable to neither: they were fine with both Marcius and his decision

compulsion: force, power

despatch: kill, or at least get rid of

suborned: bribed, induced

partisans: supporters, friends

pretense and enterprise: plot

killed him in the marketplace: Plutarch states that Marcius was killed at this time. Not all historians agree, however.

frays: quarrels

People

Aequians: or Aequi; see introductory notes for this study

Historic Occasions

488 B.C.: Possible date of the death of Coriolanus

Reading

Part One

And so remaining in camp that night, the next morning he broke up his camp, and led the Volscians homeward, variously affected with what he had done: some of them complaining of him and condemning his act; others, who were inclined to a peaceful conclusion, **unfavourable to neither**. A third party, while much disliking his proceedings, yet could not look upon Marcius as a treacherous person, but thought it pardonable in him to be thus shaken and driven to surrender at last, under such **compulsion**. None, however, opposed his commands; they all obediently followed him, though rather from admiration of his virtue than any regard they now had to his authority.

Part Two

Now the citizens of Rome plainly showed in what fear and danger their city stood of this war, when they were delivered. For so soon as the watch upon the walls of the city perceived the Volsci camp to remove, there was not a temple in the city but was presently set open, and full of men, wearing garlands of flowers upon their heads, sacrificing to the gods, as they were wont to do upon the news of some great obtained victory.

But the joy and transport of the whole city was chiefly remarkable in the honours and marks of affection paid to the women, as well by the Senate as the people in general; everyone declaring that they were, beyond all question, the instruments of the public safety. And the Senate having passed a decree that whatsoever they would ask in the way of any favour or honour should be allowed and done for them by the magistrates, they demanded simply that a temple might be erected to Female Fortune, the expense of which they offered to defray out of their own contributions, if the city would pay the cost of sacrifices, and other matters pertaining to the due honour of the gods out of the common treasury.

The Senate, much commending their public spirit, caused the temple to be built and a statue set up in it at the public charge.

[omission for length]

Part Three

When Marcius came back to Antium, Tullus, who thoroughly hated and greatly feared him, proceeded at once to contrive how he might immediately **despatch** him, as, if he escaped now, he was never likely to give him another such advantage. Having therefore got together and **suborned** several **partisans** against him, he required Marcius to resign his charge, and give the Volsci an account of his administration. Marcius, fearing to become a private man again while Tullus held the office of general and exercised the greatest power among his fellow-citizens, made answer that he was ready to lay down his commission whenever those from whose common authority he had received it should think fit to recall it; and that in the meantime he was ready to give the Antiates satisfaction as to all particulars of his conduct, if they were desirous of it.

The people hereupon called a common council, in which assembly there were certain orators appointed, that stirred up the common people against him: and when they had told their tales. But when Marcius stood up to answer, the more unruly and tumultuous part of the people became quiet on a sudden, and out of reverence, allowed him to speak without the least disturbance. Moreover, the most honest men of the Antiates, and who most rejoiced in peace, showed by their countenance that they would hear him willingly, and judge also according to their conscience. Whereupon Tullus feared that if he did let him speak, he would prove his innocence to the people, because amongst other things he had an eloquent tongue; besides that the first good service he had done to the people of the Volsci did win him more favour than these last accusations could purchase him displeasure; and furthermore, the offence they laid to his charge was a testimony of the goodwill they owed him, for they would never have thought he had done them wrong for that they took not the city of Rome, if they had not been very near taking of it, by means of his approach and conduction.

For these causes Tullus thought he might no longer delay his **pretense and enterprise**, neither to tarry for the mutinying and rising of the common people against him: wherefore, those that were of the conspiracy began to cry out that he was not to be heard, nor that they would not suffer a traitor to usurp tyrannical power over the tribe of the Volsci, who would not yield up his estate and authority.

And in saying these words, they all fell upon him, and **killed him in the marketplace**, none of those that were present offering to defend him. But it quickly appeared that the action was in nowise approved by the most part of the Volsci: for men came out of all parts to honour his body, and did honourably bury him, setting out his tomb with great store of armour and spoils, as the tomb of a worthy person and great captain.

When the Romans heard tidings of his death, they showed no other honour or malice, saving that they granted the ladies the request they made, that they might mourn ten months for him; and that was the full time they used to wear blacks for the death of their fathers, brethren, or husbands *[omission for length]*.

Part Three

Now Marcius being dead, all the Volsci heartily wished him alive again. For first of all they fell out with the **Aequians**(who were their friends and confederates) touching pre-eminence and place: and this quarrel grew on so far between them, and **frays** and murders fell out upon it one with another.

After that, the Romans overcame them in battle, in which Tullus was slain in the field, and the flower of all their force was put to the sword: so that they were forced to submit and accept of peace upon very dishonourable terms, becoming subjects of Rome, and pledging themselves to submission.

Narration and Discussion

In **Lesson One**, Plutarch quoted two common beliefs: first, that growing up (even in Rome) without a father did not prevent people from being seen as virtuous or from being respected for excellent achievements; and, second, "that a generous and worthy nature without proper discipline, like a rich soil without culture, is apt with its better fruits to produce also much that is bad and faulty." How was Coriolanus an example of both?

Creative narration: You are the head of the monument-designing committee for Coriolanus. What might it have looked like?

For older students: What is the real irony at the end of the story?

Shakespeare Connection

Again, Shakespeare plays up the drama of Aufidius' conspiracy to have Marcius assassinated. The final scene includes these lines:

> Aufidius: At a few drops of women's rheum
> *[tears]*, which are
> As cheap as lies, he sold the blood and labor
> Of our great action; therefore shall he die,
> And I'll renew me in his fall.

It's also interesting that, in the final scene, Marcius appears taken aback that the Volscians aren't pleased with his actions. He enters almost cheerfully, waving the terms of peace, and then wonders why nobody is patting him on the back. This seems to conflict with the fact that he knew he was signing his own death warrant by agreeing to the women's request; so we might think that he is just putting on a brave show here. Or maybe, in the excitement of everything, he ignored or just forgot about the danger. What do you think?

Examination Questions

Younger Students:

1. How did Marcius come to be called Coriolanus? Tell the whole story.

2. Describe the visit of Volumnia and the other Roman ladies to Marcius.

Older Students:

1. Marcius said that "by such gratifications, they did but cherish those ill seeds of boldness and petulance that had been sown among the people, which they should have done well to observe and stifle at their first appearance, and not have suffered the plebeians to grow so strong by granting them magistrates of such authority as the tribunes." Give some account of this rebellion of the people, and the behaviour of Marcius.

2. (High school) Describe and discuss the character of Gaius Marcius, as shown when he stood for the consulship after he gained the name Coriolanus.

Cato the Younger

(95-46 B.C.)

> "For he came not to serve the commonwealth to enrich himself as many did, neither for any glory or reputation, nor yet at all adventure: but that he had advisedly chosen to serve the commonwealth... and therefore thought himself bound to be as careful of his duty as the bee working her wax in the honeycomb."
>
> "And Cato himself acquired in the fullest measure what it had been his least desire to seek: glory and good repute. He was highly esteemed by all men, and entirely beloved by the soldiers. Whatever he commanded to be done, he himself took part in the performing...and he made himself, without knowing it, the object of general affection."

Marcus Porcius Cato Uticensis ("Uticensis" was added later) grew up in a world full of personal and political upheavals. He was orphaned as a baby, and a few years later the uncle who had cared for him and his siblings was murdered by political enemies; so it is no wonder that he became unusually devoted to his brother Caepio. (He is called Cato the Younger to distinguish him from his great-grandfather Cato, the subject of Plutarch's *Marcus Cato the Censor*.)

As a teenager, Cato's family connections and an enthusiastic teacher gave him a close-up view of Roman politics. He witnessed firsthand the brief but brutal period of Sulla's dictatorship, with the elimination of many "enemies." After receiving his inheritance (which allowed him to be independent), he spent his first years of young adulthood as a student of **Stoic** philosophy, with a "minimalist" lifestyle; and eventually married his first wife and started a family. In his late twenties, he began to participate in military events; commanded a legion in Macedonia; and then suffered the loss of his brother (sacrificing his usual frugality to provide him a lavish funeral). When he turned thirty, in 65 B.C., he ran successfully for **quaestor**, the position of city treasurer. (Thirty was the minimum age at that time to be elected for public office.) Two years later he became a **tribune of the people**, and had to deal with the political and legal mess caused by the Catiline Conspiracy and its aftermath. He backed Pompey's campaign in 52 B.C. to be sole **consul**, if only on the grounds that having a solid governor (even a dictator) was better than anarchy. However, he did not get along as well with Julius Caesar, and when the civil war started in 49 B.C., his loyalties were with those defending the Republic.

Cato, while respected as an administrator and an orator, was in many ways a square peg. In a time when people would do anything to gain power (change sides, bribe, send thugs to beat up political rivals, bill the government for imaginary expenses), he was more interested in upholding laws and keeping facts straight than in his own popularity. In his time as **quaestor**, he balanced the books; in his final days, while attempting to defend a town, he balanced the demands of several bickering commanders, a group of stranded senators, and three hundred Roman businessmen. The last evening of his life was spent discussing his favourite **Stoic** philosophy, particularly the idea that the "wise" or "good" man alone is free.

> "For what is liberty? The power of living as
> you please." (Cicero, *Paradoxa Stoicorum*)

Cato's Family

Cato's was first engaged to Aemilia, but lost her to Metellus Scipio, who became the target of some furious poetry, but with whom he defended Utica years later. He married a woman named Atilia and fathered Marcus Porcius Cato and Porcia; however, they were later divorced. The story of his second wife, Marcia, was unusual: a wealthy man, Hortensius, asked to marry Cato's daughter, but Porcia was both much younger than Hortensius, and was already married (to Bibulus, at that time); so Cato consented to "give" him his own wife instead. When Hortensius died, Marcia returned to Cato, partly to care for his house and younger children while he went to Sicily and then Africa to fight against Julius Caesar.

A Large Cast of Characters

Cato the Younger was related through either blood or marriage to a great number of people, and crossed paths with (seemingly) almost every famous person in late-Republic Rome. Many of them are also the subjects of Plutarch's *Lives*. Students who have already studied Pompey, Caesar, Brutus, Cicero, and/or Crassus will recognize many of the events and other characters. If this era is less familiar, be patient; parts of the story that seem unclear here will be explained more fully in other *Lives*. The **Historic Occasions** sections include notes on what people such as Caesar and Pompey were doing during Cato's lifetime, because it is sometimes important, for example, to know who was in Rome during an event and who was absent.

The Government of the Roman Republic

Commonwealth is a general term referring to a country or city/state (like Rome), and its colonies or associated territories or countries. The Roman Empire did not formally exist until Octavian (Caesar Augustus) became the first Emperor in 27 B.C. However, the Roman Republic did have an empire because of the large amount of foreign territory it was acquiring. For clarity, we will call it the small-e empire.

Social Classes

There were two different types of class divisions in ancient Rome. The first was family-based, between the **patricians** (the nobility) and the **plebeians** (common people).

The second type were property- or wealth-based classes such as the ***senatores***, the wealthiest citizens, who owned large amounts of land. The next level down, the **equestrian class** (in North's translation, the **knights of Rome**), was a "business class," made up of those who could afford horses and who therefore made up the cavalry, or soldiers on horseback, in times of war. Besides the **equestrian** class, there were three lower classes of property owners; and, lowest of all, the ***proletarii***.

Were the *senatores* the same as the senators?

Often, but the two were not identical. Over the centuries, and even within the Republic era, both the size of the Senate and the personal requirements for membership (age, wealth) changed. Some **plebeians** became senators along with the **patricians**. Those elected to **magistracies** (see below) were also included in the Senate.

What was an aedile, a quaestor, a consul?

The elected positions, or magistracies, in Rome were (starting at the bottom): quaestor, aedile, praetor, and consul. (The office of tribune was a separate position, explained below.) There were various numbers of each of these: for example, two consuls were elected each year. Ex-consuls could become censors; and a consul could become dictator if the need (usually a great emergency) arose.

Who were the tribunes?

The duty of a non-military tribune (sometimes called a tribune of the plebeians, or plebs; or a "tribune of the people") was to protect the liberties of the common people from any individual or group (such as the nobles) who might take advantage of them or suppress their rights. This position was not part of the junior-senior ranking of magistrates such as quaestor and consul; it was an office voted on by the common people (plebeians).

On the Map

Place names are listed under this heading. For consistency, I have used Dryden's spelling for places instead of North's. Charlotte Mason suggested using resources such as Dent's *Atlas of Ancient & Classical Geography*, which can be found online. A newer resource I have used myself is the *Historical Atlas of Ancient Rome* by Nick Constable (Checkmark Books/Thalamus Publishing, 2003).

Top Vocabulary Terms in Cato the Younger

If you recognize these words, you're well on your way to mastering North's vocabulary. (They will not be noted in the lessons.)

1. **bondmen:** slaves
2. **coffer:** usually a box or chest, but it is used once to refer to the treasury office
3. **divers:** several
4. **footmen:** foot soldiers. **Horse** usually refers to soldiers on horseback, or cavalry.
5. **gravity:** seriousness, particularly in attitude and manners
6. **impregnable, invincible:** unconquerable; too powerful to be defeated or destroyed
7. **marketplace:** the Forum; a place where business was conducted, speeches were made, etc. The **Capitol** was the political and religious center of Rome.
8. **prefer:** propose
9. **pulpit for orations**: place for making speeches; also called a **rostra** (Dryden's word) or rostrum
10. **recommend:** entrust, commit for safekeeping. If someone

"recommends" their children to someone else, it means "Take care of them for me" (see **Lessons Three, Eleven**).

11. **stay:** Usually means delay, detain, stop. Sometimes it means to stay in one place.

12. **talent:** a unit of money, measured by weight. A Roman talent weighed seventy-one pounds.

13. **triumph:** the parade given to honour a military hero, to show off his captives and treasure

14. **voices:** votes

Lesson One

Introduction

Plutarch says that Cato, as a tiny child, was once asked in fun by his uncle's friend Poppaedius Silo if he would support their political activism. When Cato merely gave him a *Paddington Bear*-like "hard stare," the man, still jokingly, held him out the window to make him change his mind. Plutarch says that Cato remained "unmoved and unalarmed" until Silo gave up and pulled him back in. He remarked, "What a blessing for Italy that he is but a child! If he were a man, I believe we should not gain one voice among the people."

Vocabulary

countenance: face; appearance, manner

choleric: hot-tempered

when the blood was up: when he was angered

hardly pacified: hard to calm down

a great preferment and safety...: it was a good idea to have the dictator befriend the young men, rather than view them as potential rebels or rivals

on fire with choler: red with anger

strict and austere: very plain, without luxury

priest of Apollo: one appointed to "guard the Sibylline Books." This appointment may have been influenced by the friendship between Cato's uncle Mamercus and Sulla.

Stoic: Stoicism was a school of philosophy which taught, among other things, that virtue is based on knowledge, and that the wise pay little heed to either pleasure or pain, since they can quickly change.

moral philosophy: ethics; the study of right and wrong, and how people should live

civil philosophy: political science

pricked forward: urged on

which is not to be wrought upon…: which should not be affected by personal relationships or interests

declaim: to make a speech, particularly in a loud or forceful manner

Porcian Hall: or Porcian Basilica; a large courthouse

aedile; **tribune of the people:** see introductory notes

counterfeiting fineness…: full of fine-sounding words, but lacking genuine rhetorical skill

vehemence: passion, power

obtained his cause: won his case

People

Cato the Censor; **"the old Cato":** Marcus Porcius Cato the Elder (234 B.C.–149 BC), the great-grandfather of this Cato, and the subject of Plutarch's *Marcus Cato the Censor*

Quintus Servilius Caepio: half-brother of Cato

Porcia: Cato's sister; not to be confused with his daughter, also named **Porcia**

Servilia: half-sister of Cato. He actually had two half-sisters by this name. The older one, "Servilia Major," became the mother of **Marcus Junius Brutus**, but is better known for her relationship with Julius Caesar. The younger, "Servilia Minor," became the wife of **Lucullus** (see **Lesson Two**).

(Marcus) Livius Drusus: A tribune of the people, known for his efforts at social reform. His brother **Mamercus Aemilius Lepidus Livianus** (Cato's "Uncle Mamercus") was married to **Sulla's** daughter.

Sulla: Roman general who was dictator in Rome during Cato's youth

Pompey: Gnaeus Pompeius Magnus, Roman statesman and general

Historic Occasions

106 B.C.: Births of Pompey and Cicero

100 B.C.: Birth of Julius Caesar

95 B.C.: Birth of Cato

91 B.C.: Murder of Cato's uncle Livius Drusus

91-89 B.C.: The Social War

88-85 B.C.: First Mithridatic War

85 B.C.: Birth of Marcus Junius Brutus

82/81 B.C.-79 B.C.: Sulla's dictatorship in Rome

78 B.C.: Death of Sulla

On the Map

A map of the Roman Republic, showing Italy and the lands and seas around it, would be helpful. If you are using Constable's *Historical Atlas of Ancient Rome*, there is such a map on pages 52-53.

Reading

Part One

The family and house of Cato took his first glory and name from his great grandfather, **Cato the Censor**, who for his virtue (as we have declared in his *Life*) was one of the most famous and worthiest men of Rome in his time. This Cato of whom we now write was left an orphan by his father and mother, with his brother **Caepio**, and **Porcia** his sister. **Servilia** was also Cato's half-sister, by his mother's side. All these were brought up with their uncle **Livius Drusus**, at that time the greatest man of the city: for he was passing eloquent, and very honest, and of as great a courage besides as any other Roman.

Men report that Cato from his childhood showed himself both in word and **countenance**, and also in all his pastimes and recreations, very constant and stable. For he would go through with that which he took upon him to do, and would force himself above his strength: he was rough and ungentle toward those that flattered him, and still more unyielding toward those who threatened him. He would hardly laugh, and yet had ever a pleasant countenance. He was not **choleric**, nor easy to be angered: but **when the blood was up**, he was **hardly pacified**.

When he was first put to school, he was very dull of understanding, and slow to learn: but when he had once learned it, he would never forget it, as all men else commonly do [*omission*]. It is reported that Cato was obedient unto his schoolmaster, and would do what he commanded him: howbeit he would ask him still the cause and reason of everything. Indeed his schoolmaster Sarpedon was very gentle, and readier to teach him than to strike him with his fist.

[*omission for length: Cato, even in early life, became known both for his stubbornness and his passion for justice*]

Cato at length grew so famous among (the other boys), that when **Sulla** designed to exhibit the sacred game of young men riding courses on horseback, which they called "Troy," having gotten together the youth of good birth, he (Sulla) appointed two for their leaders. One of them they accepted for his mother's sake, being the son of Metella the wife of Sulla; but as for the other, Sextus, the nephew of **Pompey,** they would not be led by him, nor exercise under him. Then Sulla asking whom they would have, they all cried out, "Cato"; and Sextus willingly yielded the honour to him, as the more worthy.

Sulla was their father's friend, and therefore did send for them many times to come unto him, and he would talk with them: the which kindness he showed to few men, for the majesty and great authority he had. Sarpedon also (Cato's schoolmaster) thinking it **a great preferment and safety for his scholars**, did commonly bring Cato into Sulla's house to wait upon him: the which was rather like unto a jail or prison, for the great number of prisoners which were daily brought thither, and put to death. Cato being then but fourteen years of age, and perceiving that there were many heads brought which were said to be of great men, and that everybody sighed and mourned to see them: he asked his schoolmaster how it was possible the tyrant escaped, that someone or other killed him not. "Because," quoth Sarpedon, "that all men fear him, more than they hate him." "Why then," replied Cato again, "didst thou not give me a sword that I might kill him, to deliver my country of this slavery and bondage?" Sarpedon hearing the boy say so, and seeing his countenance and eyes **on fire with choler**, he marvelled much at it, and afterwards had a very good eye unto him, lest rashly he should attempt something against Sulla.

When he was but a little boy, some asked him whom he loved best. "My brother," said he. Then the other continuing still to ask him, "And who next?" he answered likewise, his brother. Then the third time again, likewise, his brother. Till at length he that asked him was weary with asking him so oft.

Yea, and when he was come of age also, he then confirmed the love he bore to his brother in his deeds. For twenty years together he never supped without his brother **Caepio**, neither went he ever out of his house into the marketplace, nor into the fields without him. But when his brother made use of precious ointments and perfumes, Cato declined them; and he was, in all his habits, very **strict and austere**.

[*omission for length*]

Part Two

Cato, being made **priest of Apollo**, went to another house, took his portion of their paternal inheritance (amounting to a hundred and twenty talents), and began to live yet more strictly than before. For he fell in acquaintance with Antipater of Tyre, a **Stoic** philosopher, and gave himself chiefly unto the study of **moral and civil philosophy**, embracing all exercise of virtue with such an earnest desire that it seemed he was **pricked forward** by some god. Yet what most of all virtue and excellence fixed his affection was that steady and inflexible justice **which is not to be wrought upon by favour or compassion**. He learned also the art of speaking and debating in public, thinking that political philosophy, like a great city, should maintain for its security the military and warlike element. But he would never recite his exercises before company, nor was he ever heard to **declaim**. For when one of his friends told him one day, that men did mislike his silence, "But I hope not my life," he replied. "I will begin to speak when I have that to say which had not better be unsaid."

Part Three

The great **Porcian Hall**, as it was called, had been built and dedicated to the public use by **the old Cato**, when **aedile**. Here the **tribunes of the people** used to transact their business, and because one of the pillars was thought to interfere with the convenience of their seats, they deliberated whether it were best to remove it to another place, or to take it away. That was the first cause that made Cato, against his will, to go into the marketplace, and to get up into the pulpit for orations, to speak against them: where having given this first proof of his eloquence and noble mind, he was marvellously esteemed of. For his oration was not like a young man, **counterfeiting fineness of speech and affectation**, but stout, full of wit and **vehemence**: and yet in the shortness of his sentences, he had such an excellent grace withal, that he marvellously delighted the hearers: and furthermore, showing in nature a certain gravity besides, it did so please them, that he made them laugh. He had a very full and audible voice that might be heard of a marvellous number of people, and such a strong nature besides, that he never fainted, nor broke his speech: for many times he would speak a whole day together, and was never weary.

So when he had **obtained his cause** against the tribunes, he returned again to keep his former great silence, and to harden his body with painful exercises, as to abide heat, frost, and snow bareheaded; and always to go afoot in the field, where his friends that did accompany him rode a-horseback, and sometime he would come and talk with one, sometimes with another, as he went afoot by them.

[*omission for length*]

Narration and Discussion

Tell what you know of Cato's childhood, both what he was like and the world around him. You may want to "interview" someone who grew up with Cato.

Why did Cato's teacher take his show of emotion over Sulla very seriously?

For older students: " Yet what most of all virtue and excellence fixed his affection was that steady and inflexible justice which is not to be wrought upon by favour or compassion." How have we seen this already in Cato's life? Watch for more examples as the story goes on.

Creative narration: This lesson offers several possibilities for writing dialogue or acting out scenes. (Hanging anyone out the window is not allowed.)

Lesson Two

Introduction

From philosophy student to army commander: while still a young man, Cato successfully managed a military legion (approximately five thousand soldiers and their officers), and his reputation reached the ears of General Pompey. When he returned to Rome, he had lost his brother, but had gained a new friend, the philosopher Athenodorus.

Vocabulary

blow into their ears…: boost their public image by appearing able to greet all the voters by name

practised: planned, plotted

lenity: gentleness

lost labour: a waste of time

cavil: object, complain

obsequies: funeral rites

time of his charge was expired: term of duty in Macedon was finished

no better colour nor occasion: no better excuse

veneration: reverence, respect

keep back: retain, keep with him

People

Julius Caesar: Roman politician and general

Spartacus: a gladiator turned rebel and military leader

Gellius: Lucius Gellius Publicola, consul in 72 B.C.

Rubrius: praetor in Macedon probably from 69-67 B.C.

Athenodorus (surnamed Cordylion): philosopher and librarian at Pergamum. It is said that he was accused of having cut out portions of a philosophy book with which he disagreed, and was ordered to paste it back together.

Lucullus: Lucius Lucinius Lucullus, a Roman general who had been a confederate of Sulla; the subject of Plutarch's *Lucullus*. He was also Cato's brother-in-law.

King Deiotarus: a king in western Galatia (now part of Turkey)

Historic Occasions

75 B.C.: Julius Caesar travelled to Rhodes and was kidnapped by pirates (see the *Life of Julius Caesar)*

ca. 73 B.C.: Cato married Atilia

72 B.C.: Rebellion of slaves led by Spartacus

70 B.C.: Crassus and Pompey were consuls

69 B.C.: Julius Caesar was quaestor and served in Hispania

67 B.C.: Caesar returned to Rome and re-entered politics

67 B.C.: Cato sent to Macedon as a tribune; his brother Caepio died during that time

On the Map

Macedon: or Macedonia; a kingdom to the north of Greece, which had become a Roman province

Pergamum: or Pergamon/Pergamos; city in the region of Mysia

Asia: The Roman province of Asia consisted of the former kingdoms of Mysia, Lydia, and others.

Aenus in Thrace: Or Enez; an ancient city, now part of Turkey

Thessaly: a region of Greece which became part of **Macedonia**

Ephesus: Greek city, now part of Turkey.

Reading

Part One

In the war of the slaves, which took its name from **Spartacus** (their ringleader), **Gellius** was general; and Cato went as a volunteer, for the sake of his brother Caepio, who was a tribune in the army. Cato could find here no opportunity to show his zeal or exercise his valour, on account of the ill conduct of the general. However, amidst the corruption and disorders of that army, he showed such a love of discipline, so much bravery upon occasion, and so much courage and wisdom in everything, that it appeared he was in no way inferior to the old Cato. Gellius offered him great rewards, and would have decreed him the first honours; which, however, he refused, saying he had done nothing that deserved them. This made him to be thought a man of strange and eccentric temper.

Furthermore, when there was a law made, forbidding all men that sued for any office in the commonwealth, that they should have no prompters, in any of the assemblies, **to blow into their ears the names of private citizens**: he alone, when he sued to be elected tribune, was obedient to the law, and committed all the private citizens' names to memory, to speak unto every one of them, and to call them by their names: so that he was envied even by those that did commend him. For the more they considered the excellence of what he did, the more they were grieved at the difficulty they found to do the like.

So Cato being elected tribune, he was sent into **Macedon**, unto **Rubrius**, who was praetor there [*omission*]. He had fifteen slaves with him, two free men, and four of his friends, which rode, and he himself went afoot, sometimes talking with one, otherwhile with another as he went. When he came to the camp, where there were many legions of the Romans, the praetor immediately gave him charge of one of them: who, thinking it small honour to him for himself only to be valiant, since he was but one man, he **practised** to make all his soldiers under him like unto himself. The which he did not by fear and terror, but by **lenity** and gentle persuasion, training and instructing them in every point what they should do: adding to his gentle instruction and persuasions, reward to those that did well, and punishment to them that offended. Whereby it was hard to judge whether he had made them more quiet than warlike and more valiant than just: so dreadful they showed themselves to their enemies, and courteous to their friends; fearful to do evil, and ready to win honour.

And Cato himself acquired in the fullest measure what it had been his least desire to seek: glory and good repute. He was highly esteemed by all men, and entirely beloved by the soldiers. Whatever he commanded to be done, he himself took part in the performing; in his apparel, his diet, and mode of travelling, he was more like a common soldier than an officer; but in character, high purpose, and wisdom, he far exceeded all that had the names and titles of commanders, and he made himself, without knowing it, the object of general affection. For the true love of virtue, (to wit, the desire to follow it) taketh no root in men's minds, unless they have a singular love and reverence unto the person, whom they desire to follow.

Part Two

When Cato understood that **Athenodorus (surnamed Cordylion)**, a Stoic philosopher, excellently well learned, dwelt at that time in the city of **Pergamum**, being a very old man, and one that stiffly refused the friendship of princes and great men, he was desirous to have him about them; but to write to him, he thought it was but **lost labour**. Wherefore having two months' liberty by the laws of the Romans to follow his own affairs, he took sea, and went into **Asia** to him, hoping he should not lose his journey, for the great virtues he knew to be in him. So when he had spoken with him, and talked of divers matters together: at length he brought him from his first determination, and carried him to the camp with him, esteeming this victory more than all the conquests of **Lucullus** or Pompey, who had conquered the most part of all the provinces and realms of the Eastern parts of the world.

While Cato was yet in the service, his brother, on a journey towards Asia, fell sick at **Aenus in Thrace**; letters with intelligence of which were immediately dispatched to him. Cato took sea presently, when it was marvellous rough and boisterous, and embarked in a small trading-vessel of a merchant of **Thessaly**, with two of his friends, and three bondmen only, and did escape drowning very narrowly; and yet by good fortune arrived safely, a little after his brother Caepio's death. He took his death more sorrowfully than became a philosopher, not only mourning and lamenting for him, embracing the dead corpse of his brother: but also for the exceeding charge and sumptuous funerals, which he bestowed upon him, in perfumes, sweet savours, and sumptuous silks that were burnt with his body: and furthermore, in the stately tomb of Thracian marble which he made for him, and set up in the marketplace of the Aenians, that cost eight talents.

For there were some who took upon them to **cavil** at all this as not consistent with his usual calmness and moderation, not discerning that though he were steadfast, firm, and inflexible to pleasure, fear or foolish entreaties, yet he was full of natural tenderness and brotherly affection. Divers cities, princes and noblemen sent him many sundry presents, to honour the funerals of his brother Caepio; howbeit, he took no money of all them, saving only spices, and sweet savours, and such other ornaments as honoured the **obsequies** of the dead; and yet he paid for them, unto those that brought them, as much as they were worth.

[*omission for length*]

So when Cato's **time of his charge was expired**, they did accompany him at his departure, not only with ordinary praises, vows, and prayers to the gods for his health: but with embracing, tears, and marvelous lamentations of the soldiers, which spread their garments on the ground as he went, and kissing of his hands, which honour the Romans did but to very few of their generals.

Part Three

Furthermore, Cato being determined, before he returned to Rome to deal in the affairs there, to go and see Asia, partly to be an eyewitness of the manners, customs, and power of every province as he went; and partly also to satisfy **King Deiotarus'** request, who having been his father's friend, had earnestly entreated him to come and see him: he went the journey, and used it in this sort. First, by peep of day, he sent his baker and cook before, where he meant to lie that night. They, coming soberly into the city or village, inquired if there were none of Cato's friends and acquaintance there, and if they found none, then they prepared his supper in an inn, and troubled no man; but if there were no inn, then they went to the governors of the town, and prayed them to help them to lodging, and did content themselves with the first that was offered them. Oftentimes the townsmen did not believe they were Cato's men, and made no account of them: because they took all things so quietly, and made no ado with the officers. Insomuch as Cato sometimes came himself, and found nothing ready for him, and when he was come, they made as small account of him, seeing him set upon his carriages, and speak never a word: for they took him for some mean man, and a timorous person. Notwithstanding, sometime he called them unto him, and told them, "O poor men, learn to be more courteous to receive travelling Romans that pass by you, and look not always to have Catos to come unto you; and therefore see that you use them with such courtesy and entertainment, that they may bridle the authority they have over you: for you shall find many that will desire **no better colour nor occasion** by force to take from you that which they would have, because you unwillingly also do grant them the things they would, and need."

[*omission for length*]

Part Four

Cato, arriving at the city of **Ephesus**, went towards Pompey to salute him, being the elder man, and of greater dignity and estimation than he, who at that time also was general of a great and powerful army. Pompey, seeing him coming towards him afar off, would not tarry till he came to him, sitting in his chair of state; but, rising up went to meet him, as one of the greatest and noblest persons of Rome; and taking him by the hand, after he had embraced and welcomed him, he presently fell in praise of his virtue before his face, and afterwards also commended him in his absence, when he was gone from him. Whereupon, every man after that had him in great **veneration** for those things which before they despised in him, when they considered better of his noble and courteous mind. For men that saw Pompey's entertainment towards him, knew well enough that Cato was a man which he rather reverenced, and for a kind of duty observed, more than for any love he bore him; and they noted further that he honoured him greatly while he was with him, but yet that he was glad when Cato went from him. For he sought to **keep back** all the young gentlemen of Rome that went to see him, and desired them to remain with him: but for Cato, he was nothing desirous of his company, for that in his presence he thought he could not command as he would, and therefore was willing to let him go, recommending his wife and his children to him, the which he never did before unto any other Roman that returned to Rome; and he was indeed connected by relationship with Cato.

Narration and Discussion

How did Cato achieve "glory and good repute" without seeming to want them?

Plutarch says that Pompey "honoured him greatly while he was with him, but yet that he was glad when Cato went from him." Why?

Creative narration #1: Act out the story about showing hospitality to strangers. (Christian students may want to look up Hebrews 13:2.)

Creative narration #2: You are one of the soldiers in Cato's legion, and you have been asked to make a speech at his farewell dinner. What will you say?

For extra credit: Cato had an amazing knack for remembering people's names (and, considering how repetitive Roman names could be, that was no mean feat). Why is that a useful skill? What are some ways to improve one's memory for things like names? Have you tried any of them?

Lesson Three

Introduction

As Cato made his way back to Rome, he was feasted in every town, and offered gifts by a king who wanted protection. This made his Stoic soul very nervous, to the point that he asked his friends to keep reminding him of a comment, made half-jokingly, that the trip through Asia might soften him up. Having weathered those temptations and returned home, he took on a government position for which he seemed perfectly suited: a **quaestor**, or manager of the Roman treasury. Those used to an easy time in the accounting department were in for a surprise.

Vocabulary

strove and emulated each other: tried to outdo each other

familiar: friend

corruption would never want pretense: North, "otherwise, corruption and bribery could lack no honest colour to take." To use Charlotte Mason's vocabulary, the Way of Reason can always find an excuse for accepting a bribe.

breach of trust: If someone entrusts you with goods or information, or trusts you to do something, and you do not keep those things safe or do what was asked, you have committed a breach of trust.

intimate with Cato: a good friend, used in the same sense as **familiar**

So perceiving he could not bring off his client…: Seeing that he had no chance of winning in a trial, he tried to "settle out of court."

litter: bed or chair that can be carried

pride and stomach: arrogance, boastfulness

he would not admit of it: he would not accept the new order (until he had verified that it actually was passed by vote)

the coffer of the treasurers: the treasury office

friends that were importunate: people that kept bothering them

pass a certain debt to the public revenue…: they were trying to take money from the treasury to pay off personal debts

People

Athenodorus: see previous lesson

Lutatius Catulus: Quintus Lutatius Catulus Capitolinus (ca. 120 B.C.-59 B.C.); a former consul

Marcellus: Marcus Claudius Marcellus; believed to be the Marcellus who was consul in 51 B.C.

Historic Occasions

65 B.C.: Cato returned to Rome and was elected quaestor

65 B.C.: Crassus was censor

On the Map

Pessinus: a city in Asia Minor (Asia Minor is also called Anatolia, or Asian Turkey)

Brundisium: or Brindisi; a port on the Adriatic Sea

Reading

Part One

After this, all the cities through which he passed **strove and emulated each other** in showing him respect and honour, and made him great feasts and banquets: in the which he prayed his friends to have an eye to him, least unawares he should prove Curio's words true. For Curio sometimes being his friend, and a **familiar** of his (though misliking his severity), asked Cato if he would go see Asia, when he left the army. Cato answered again that it was his full determination. "You do well," replied Curio, "you will bring back with you a better temper and pleasanter manners."

Furthermore, Deiotarus the king of Galatia, being a very old man, sent for Cato to come into his country to recommend his sons and house to his protection: who, when he arrived there, had great rich presents of all sorts offered him by the king, entreating him all he could to take them. This so much misliked and angered Cato, that though he came in the evening, he stayed only that night, and went away early the next morning. After he was gone one day's journey, he found at **Pessinus** a yet greater quantity of presents provided for him there, and also letters from Deiotarus entreating him to receive them, or at least to permit his friends to take them, who for his sake deserved some gratification, and could not have much done for them out of Cato's own means. Yet he would not suffer it, though he saw some of them very willing to receive such gifts, and ready to complain of his severity; but he answered that **corruption would never want pretense**, and his friends should share with him in whatever he should justly and honestly obtain; and so he returned the presents to Deiotarus.

Part Two

Now when he was ready to embark, to pass over the sea again unto **Brundisium**, his friends would have persuaded him to put his brother's ashes into another vessel. But he answered them, that he would rather lose his own life than to leave his brother's relics. Thereupon he presently hoisted sail, and it is reported that he passed over in great danger, where other ships arrived very safely.

After he was returned to Rome, he spent his time for the most part either at home, in conversation with **Athenodorus**, or at the Forum, in the service of his friends. Though it was now the time that he should become quaestor, he would not stand for the place till he had studied the laws relating to it, and by inquiry from persons of experience, had attained a distinct understanding of the duty and authority belonging to it.

So he no sooner came to his office, but he presently made great alteration amongst the clerks and officers of the treasury [*omission*]. Cato, applying himself roundly to the work, showed that he possessed not only the title and honour of a quaestor, but the knowledge and understanding and full authority of his office. Thus, he used the clerks and under-officers like servants as they were, exposing their corrupt practices, and instructing their ignorance. Being bold, impudent fellows, they flattered the other quaestors, his colleagues, and by their means endeavoured to maintain an opposition against him. But he convicted the chiefest of them of a **breach of trust** in the charge of an inheritance, and turned him out of his place. A second he brought to trial for dishonesty, who was defended by **Lutatius Catulus**, at that time censor, a man very considerable for his office, but yet more for his character, as he was eminent above all the Romans of that age for his reputed wisdom and integrity. He was also **intimate with Cato**, and much commended his way of living. **So perceiving he could not bring off his client if he stood a fair trial, he openly began to beg him off.** Cato objected to his doing this. Cato plainly said unto him,

"It is a shame for thee, Catulus, thou that art censor, and shouldest reform all our lives, thus to forget the duty of thine office, to please our ministers." Catulus looking at Cato when he had spoken, as though he would answer him: whether it were for shame, or anger, he went his way, and said never a word more. Yet was not the party condemned, though there was one voice more that did condemn than clear him, because of the absence of one of the judges. For Marcus Lollius, one of Cato's colleagues in the quaestorship, being sick at that time and absent, Catulus sent unto him to pray him to come and help the poor man. Thereupon Lollius being brought thither in a **litter** after judgement given, gave his last voice, which absolutely cleared him. (Cato, this notwithstanding, would never use him as a clerk, nor pay him his wages, nor would count of Lollius' vote among others.)

Part Three

Thus having pulled down the **pride and stomach** of these clerks, and brought them unto reason: in short time he had all the tables and records at his commandment, and made the treasure chamber as honourable as the Senate itself: so that every man thought, and said, that Cato had added unto the quaestorship the dignity of the consulship. For finding divers men indebted before unto the commonwealth, and the commonwealth also unto divers men: he set down such an order, that the public might no longer either do or suffer wrong. For being rough with them that were indebted to the chamber, he compelled them to pay their debt, and willingly and quickly also paid them to whom the chamber owed anything: so that the people were ashamed to see some pay which never thought to have paid anything, and on the contrary side also there were others paid, which never looked to have had any part of their debts paid them. And whereas usually those who brought false bills and pretended orders of the senate could through favour get them accepted, Cato would never be so imposed upon; and in the case of one particular order, on the question arising whether it had passed the senate, he would not believe a great many witnesses that attested it, nor **would admit of it**, till the consuls came and affirmed it upon oath.

[*omission for length*]

Besides all this, Cato's continual pains and care of the treasure, was so well thought of, and liked of the people, as could be. For he was always the first that came to **the coffer of the treasurers**, and also the last that went from thence, and was never weary of any pains. Furthermore, he never missed to be at any assembly of the people or Senate, fearing, and being always careful, lest lightly by favour, any money due to the commonwealth should be forgiven: or else that they should abate the rent of the farmers, or that they should give no money but to them that had justly deserved it. Thus having rid all accusers, and also filled the coffers with treasure, he made men see that the commonwealth might be rich without oppressing of any man. Indeed at his first coming in to the office, his colleagues and companions found him marvellous troublesome and tedious, for that they thought him too rough and severe: howbeit they all loved him in the end, because he only withstood the complaints and cries of all men against them (which complained that they would not for any man's respect or favour let go the money of the common treasure) and was contented his companions should excuse themselves unto their **friends that were importunate**, and lay the fault upon him, saying, that it was impossible for them to bring Cato unto it.

The last day that he went out of his office, being very honourably brought home to his house by the people: it was told him that several powerful friends were in the treasury with the other quaestor, **Marcellus**, using all their interest with him to **pass a certain debt to the public revenue, as if it had been a gift**. This Marcellus had been Cato's friend even from their childhood, and whilst Cato was in office, he did orderly execute his office with him: but when he was left alone, he was of so gentle a nature, that he would easily be entreated, and was as much ashamed to deny any man, as he was also overready to grant every man that he required. Cato straight returned back upon it, and finding that Marcellus had yielded to pass the thing, he took the book, and while Marcellus silently stood by and looked on, struck it out. This done, he brought Marcellus out of the treasury, and took him home with him; who for all this, neither then, nor ever after, complained of him, but always continued his friendship and familiarity with him.

Narration and Discussion

How did Cato's experiences in Asia prepare him for his new position?

How did Cato "make the treasure chamber as honourable as the Senate itself?" (Bible verse to look up: Proverbs 20:10)

For older students: How did Cato balance law with mercy in the case of Marcellus?

For older students: One of Cato's goals as quaestor was that "the commonwealth might be rich without oppressing of any man." Is that possible?

Creative narration: Write or act out a conversation between two clerks in the Roman treasury office. One of them likes Cato's new work atmosphere, and the other wishes for the good old days.

Lesson Four

Introduction

Note: The next two lessons are "Part A" and "Part B" of the same story. You could choose to divide them slightly differently.

We begin with a reminder that Cato wanted only "to serve the commonwealth, like a just and honest man," and that he made a point of studying not only the laws of Rome, but everything done by the governors of its overseas provinces. In our day, he might be the political science professor who appears on the news to comment on state decisions and foreign affairs; or perhaps someone with his own podcast. He gained a reputation for being the most-believed person in Rome.

In the years leading up to Caesar's civil war, there were several disturbances and good reasons to worry. Pompey, who had been fighting overseas, was expected to return to Rome soon, and his popularity and power were growing even in his absence. In the meantime, he appeared to be sending "minions," such as Metellus Nepos, to run for office and promote his interests. Cato, in the interest of stability, agreed to run for tribune himself.

In the same year, the consul Cicero uncovered a plot (called the **Catiline Conspiracy**) to overthrow the government and burn down the city. This story can be read elsewhere (including Plutarch's *Cicero*); but one of the important aftershocks was a high level of anger and blame, both for those leaders who acted perhaps too quickly to suppress the conspiracy, and those who seemed to support it (or who attempted to protect their friends) by their lack of action. Metellus, who had just begun his time as tribune along with Cato, did everything he could to make Cicero's last month in office a miserable one. (New tribunes began their work in December, but consuls did not change until January.) He also created a bill, to be voted in by the people, to allow Pompey, plus military backup as required, to have full power to protect Rome from civil unrest.

But even the voting was not going to be easy.

Vocabulary

laid down his office: stopped being quaestor

consort: crony, supporter

compel: force

win or corrupt: bribe

matters of arbitration: cases where his help was supposedly needed

traduced to the people: publicly accused

infamous: known for bad deeds

betimes: early; first thing in the morning

cross Metellus' enterprise: interfere with his plans

carry it from them all: defeat their proposal

favour his suit: support his campaign

bewray: reveal

insinuated and charged against him in the senate: he was accused of showing favouritism over the conspiracy issue

the most corrupt and dissolute elements of the state: North puts it "rakehells and seditious persons," or troublemakers and rebels

fair pretense: official version, cover story

entreaty: pleading

extolled: praised

insolent: proud, arrogant

ecstasy of contention: something like "getting carried away trying to be Super-Virtue-Man"

People

Clodius: Publius Clodius Pulcher. Roman politician, known for his long-running feud with Cicero.

Cicero: Marcus Tullius Cicero, Roman statesman, lawyer, and philosopher; consul for 63 B.C.

Metellus Nepos: Quintus Caecilius Metellus Nepos (100 B.C.-55 B.C.). Tribune for 62 B.C., praetor in 60 B.C., and consul in 57 B.C. Another enemy of Cicero.

Lentulus: Publius Cornelius Lentulus Sura, a former consul; involved in the Catiline Conspiracy; put to death with others in December 63 B.C.

Lucius Sergius Catilina: or Catiline. An unsuccessful candidate for consul of the previous year, and the leader of a plot to overthrow the government

Historic Occasions

63 B.C.: Cato divorced Atilia and married Marcia

63 B.C.: Cicero was consul; Caesar was *Pontifex Maximus* (chief priest)

63 B.C.: Cato and Metellus Nepos elected as "tribunes of the people," and Caesar elected praetor (taking office in December for the following year)

November 63 B.C.: The Catiline conspiracy was exposed by Cicero; Catiline fled from Rome, where he died in battle soon afterwards.

December 63 B.C.: Lentulus and other conspirators were put to death for their part in the Catiline Conspiracy; Caesar argued for imprisonment, but Cato's speech led to their execution.

Reading

Part One

Cato, after he had **laid down his office**, yet did not cease to keep a watch upon the treasury. He had his servants who continually wrote out the details of the expenditure, and he himself kept always by him certain books, which contained the accounts of the revenue from Sulla's time to his own quaestorship, which he had bought for five talents. He was the first man that came to the Senate, and the last that went out of it. There many times, the senators tarrying long before they came, he went and sat down in a corner by himself, and read closely the book he had under his gown, clapping his gown before it; and he would never be out of the city on that day when he knew the Senate should assemble.

After that, Pompey and his **consorts** perceiving that it was impossible to **compel** Cato, and much less to **win or corrupt** him, to favour their unjust doings: they sought what means they could to keep him from coming to the Senate, by asking him to defend certain of his friends' causes, and occupying him some other ways about **matters of arbitration**. But he quickly discovered the trick, and, to defeat it, fairly told all his acquaintance that he would never meddle in any private business when the Senate was assembled.

For he came not to serve the commonwealth to enrich himself as many did, neither for any glory or reputation, nor yet at all adventure: but that he had advisedly chosen to serve the commonwealth, like a just and honest man, and therefore thought himself bound to be as careful of his duty as the bee working her wax in the honeycomb. For this respect therefore, to perform his duty the better, by the means of his friends, which he had in every province belonging to the empire of Rome, he got into his hands the copies of all the chiefest acts, edicts, decrees, sentences, and the notablest judgements of the governors that remained in record.

Once when **Clodius**, the seditious orator, to promote his violent and revolutionary projects, **traduced to the people** some of the priests and priestesses (among whom Fabia, sister to **Cicero's** wife Terentia, ran great danger), Cato, having boldly interfered, and having made Clodius appear so **infamous** that he was forced to leave the town, was addressed, when it was over, by Cicero, who came to thank him for what he had done. "You must thank the commonwealth," said he, for whose sake alone he professed to do everything.

Hereby Cato won him great fame. For when a certain orator or common councillor preferred one witness unto the judges, the councillor on the other side told them, that one witness was not to be credited, though it were Cato himself. Insomuch as the people took it up for a proverb among them, that when any man spoke any strange and unlikely matter, they would say: "Nay, though Cato himself said it, yet were it not to be believed."

Part Two

[*Omission for length: Cato's friends wanted him to run for the office of "tribune of the people," but he at first did not see the need to take on such a position. While heading out of the city for a vacation, however, he received the news that* ***Metellus Nepos*** *was running for the same position, and he immediately ordered the whole company to turn around.*]

Cato said, "Do not you know that Metellus is to be feared of himself, for his rashness and folly; and now that he cometh instructed by Pompey, like a lightning he would set all the commonwealth afire? For this cause therefore, we must not now go take our pleasure in the country, but overcome his folly, or otherwise die honourably in defense of our liberty." Yet at his friends' persuasions, he went first unto his house in the country, but tarried not long there, and returned straight again to Rome.

When he came thither overnight, the next morning **betimes** he went into the marketplace, and sued to be tribune of the people, purposely to **cross Metellus' enterprise**; because the power and authority of the tribune consisteth more in hindering, than in *doing* anything: for if all men else were agreed of a matter, and that he only were against it, the tribune would **carry it from them all**.

Cato at the first had not many of his friends about him; but when they heard of his intent, why he made suit for the tribuneship: all his friends and noblemen straight took part with him, confirmed his determination, and encouraged him to go on withal, for that he did it rather to serve the commonwealth, than his own turn, considering, that where many times before he might (without resistance or denial) have obtained the same, the state being toward no trouble, he then would never sue for it, but now that he saw it in danger, where he was to fight for the commonwealth, and the protection of her liberty. It is reported that there was such a number of people about him to **favour his suit**, that he was like to have been stifled among them, and thought he should never have come to the marketplace, for the press of people that swarmed about him.

Thus when he was chosen tribune with Metellus and others, he perceived how they bought and sold the voices of the people when the consuls were chosen: whereupon he made an oration, and sharply rebuked the people for this corruption; and after his oration ended, solemnly protested by oath that he would accuse anyone, and **bewray** his name, which had given money to be chosen consul.

Part Three

[*Omission for length: the Catiline Conspiracy, and the marriage troubles of Cato*]

Lentulus and the rest of the conspirators were put to death; but Caesar, finding so much **insinuated and charged against him in the senate**, betook himself to the people, and proceeded to stir up **the most corrupt and dissolute elements of the state** to form a party in his support. Whereupon Cato, fearing lest such rabble of people should put all the commonwealth in uproar and danger: he persuaded the

Senate to win the poor needy people that had nothing, by distributing of corn amongst them, the which was done: for the charge thereof amounted yearly unto twelve hundred and fifty talents. This liberality did manifestly drink up and quench all those troubles which they stood in fear of.

But on the other side, Metellus Nepos, entering into his tribuneship, made certain seditious orations and assemblies, and proposed a law to the people that Pompey the Great should presently be called into Italy with his army, so that he should keep the city by his coming from the present danger of Catiline's conspiracy. This was the **fair pretense**; but the true design was to deliver all into the hands of Pompey, and to give him an absolute power.

Upon this the Senate was assembled, and Cato did not fall sharply upon Metellus, as he often did, but urged his advice in the most reasonable and moderate tone. At least he descended even to **entreaty**, and **extolled** the house of Metellus as having always taken part with the nobility. At this Metellus grew the more **insolent**, and despising Cato, as if he yielded and were afraid, let himself proceed to make proud speeches against him, and cruel threats, that in despite of the Senate he would do that which he had undertaken. Then Cato, changing his countenance, his voice and speech, after he had spoken very sharply against him: in the end he roughly protested that while he lived, he would never suffer Pompey to come into Rome with his army. The senate thought them both extravagant, and not well in their safe senses; for the design of Metellus seemed to be mere rage and frenzy, out of excess of mischief bringing all things to ruin and confusion; and Cato's virtue looked like a kind of **ecstasy of contention** in the cause of what was good and just.

But when the day came for the people to give their voices for the passing of this decree, and Metellus beforehand occupied the Forum with armed men, strangers, gladiators, and slaves, those that in hopes of change followed Pompey were known to be no small part of the people, and besides, they had great assistance from Caesar, who was then praetors; and though the best and chiefest men of the city were no less offended at these proceedings than Cato, they seemed rather likely to suffer with him than able to assist him. The night before, Cato's friends in their own homes, and his whole family, were marvellously perplexed and sorrowful, that they both refused their meat, and also could take no rest in the night because they feared for Cato. But he, as one without fear, having a good heart with him, did comfort his people, and bade them not sorrow for him: and after he had supped, as he commonly used to do, he went to bed, and slept soundly all night till the morning, when Minucius Thermus, his colleague and fellow tribune, came and called him.

Narration and Discussion

Why was Cato at first reluctant to run for the position of tribune? Why did he change his mind?

Considering their friendly meeting earlier (**Lesson Two)**, why would Cato *not* want Pompey to come into Rome with an army?

Creative narration: Create campaign posters for Cato and the other candidates for tribune.

Lesson Five

Introduction

Having irritated everyone around him with his calmness (what else would they have expected?), Cato headed off to the Forum for the voting and the expected riots.

After this tumultuous time, Cato seemed to stand, if briefly, in a position where he could press his own political ideas, rid himself of personal enemies such as Metellus Nepos, and even ingratiate himself forever with Pompey by approving a double marriage match within their families. However (what else would they have expected?), Cato followed his own set of values.

Vocabulary

naked: that is, unprotected

asunder: separated

without book: without needing to read it; by heart

sedition: rebellion

vehemently bent…: passionately determined to follow through on his plan

peradventure: perhaps

he presently departed Rome: As a tribune of the people, he was breaking the rules by leaving the city.

infamy: criminal acts

Pompey had taken the honour…: Pompey had replaced Lucullus as commander in the Third Mithridatic War, in response to which Lucullus called him a "vulture."

bulwark: defensive wall

favour Piso's suit, suing to be consul: Pompey wanted to support Piso's election campaign

devices: tricks, plots

he sent a great sum of money…: This incident is described in Plutarch's *Pompey*

in Pompey's own garden: the garden was a rather exposed location for exchanging bribe money

matching: political alliance

both the one and the other…: they had struggled over who gave the orders

the law for dividing of the lands amongst the soldiers: Also called the *lex agraria* or the law Agraria, a bill to make land available to needy citizens and returning soldiers. The proposed law itself, although controversial, is not the point; the three-year attempt to pass or kill it was the symbol of the larger power struggle in the Roman Senate.

was the only author: was to blame

People

Lucius Lucinius Murena: see **Historic Occasions**

Gaius Memmius: Orator and poet; tribune in 66 B.C.

Piso: lieutenant to Pompey. Pompey requested that the elections be postponed to allow for Piso's late entry into the contest.

Munatius: Munatius Rufus; a close friend of Cato, and a source for later biographers

Historic Occasions

66 B.C.: Lucullus returned from the Third Mithridatic War, and was given a triumph (three years later)

62 B.C.: Lucius Licinius Murena was consul, but was put on trial for election bribery, and was defended by Crassus and Cicero

62 B.C.: Pompey returned to Italy, but not yet to Rome

62 B.C.: Piso elected consul for the following year

December 62 B.C.: Clodius was at the center of what was called the *Bona Dea* scandal, which is detailed in other *Lives.* His trial dragged on for months, until he was finally acquitted due to the financial influence of Crassus.

September 61 B.C.: Pompey entered Rome for his third triumph

Reading

Part One

So they both went together into the marketplace, accompanied with a very few people after them; whereupon divers of their friends came and met them by the way, and bade them take heed unto themselves. When they were come into the marketplace, and Cato saw the Temple of Castor and Pollux full of armed men, and the steps or passages kept by gladiators, and Metellus on the top of them seated by Caesar:

turning to his friends he said, "See I pray you the coward there, what a number of armed men he hath gotten together, against one man **naked** and unarmed." Therewithal he straight went forward with his companion Thermus unto that place, and they that kept the passages opened of themselves to let him pass; but they would let no other go up but himself. But Cato with much ado, taking Minucius by the hand, got him up with him, and when he was come up, he sat him down betwixt Metellus and Caesar, to keep them **asunder**, that they should not whisper one in another's ear, at which they were both amazed and confounded. Whereupon the noblemen that considered Cato's countenance and boldness, wondering to see it, drew near; and by their cries willed him not to be afraid, but encouraged one another to stick by him, that stood for defense of their liberty.

So, there was a servant that took the written law in his hand, and would have read it to the people: but Cato would not let him. Then Metellus took it himself in his hands to read it: but Cato also snatched it out of his hands. Metellus notwithstanding, having it perfect **without book**, would needs declare the effect of it by heart. But Thermus clapped his hand before his mouth to keep him that he should not speak. Metellus seeing these two men bent by all means to keep this law from passing, and that the people did lean on their side: he beckoned to his men to go for the armed men which were at home in his house, that they should come with terror and cries to make them afraid, and so they did.

The people thereupon were dispersed here and there for fear, so that Cato was left alone in the marketplace; and they threw stones at him from beneath. But then **Lucius Lucinius Murena**, who had before been accused by Cato for buying of the consulship, forsook him not in that danger, but holding his long gown before him, cried out unto them beneath, that threw at Cato, to leave. So showing him the danger he had brought himself unto, holding him still by the arms, he brought Cato into the Temple of Castor and Pollux.

Then Metellus seeing the pulpit for orations empty, and his enemies fleeing out of the marketplace, he thought he had won the goal; whereupon, commanding his soldiers to depart, then proceeding gently, he attempted to pass his law. But his enemies that fled for fear, being gathered again together in the marketplace, began afresh to cry out against Metellus, with greater boldness and courage than before.

Then Metellus and his adherents being afraid and amazed, doubting that their enemies had gotten weapons, and were provided, and therefore were the bolder: they fled, and all of them left the pulpit for orations.

So, when Metellus and his company were gone, Cato came again to the pulpit for orations, and greatly commended the people for the goodwill they had shown, and persuaded them to continue in their well-doing. Whereupon the common people were then against Metellus; and the Senate, also being assembled, gave order that Cato should have better aid than he had before, and that by all means possible they should resist Metellus' law, which only tended to move **sedition** and civil war in Rome. For Metellus himself, he was yet **vehemently bent to follow his attempt and enterprise**: but perceiving that his friends were marvellously afraid of Cato, as a man whom they thought invincible, he suddenly came into the marketplace, and assembling the people, told them many reasons in his oration, supposing to bring Cato in disgrace with the people; and amongst other things he said was that he would withdraw himself out of this tyrannical power of Cato's, and his conspiracy against Pompey, the which **peradventure** the city, before it were long, should repent for that they had shamed and defaced so noble a man.

After that, **he presently departed Rome,** and went into Asia to inform Pompey of all this matter.

Part Two

Cato on the other side was greatly esteemed for his doings, for that he had freed the commonwealth from the great trouble of such a foolish tribune, and by overthrowing Metellus, he had also suppressed the power of Pompey. But he was yet much more commended when he was against the Senate, who would have accused Metellus of **infamy**, and deprived him of his office, the which he would not suffer them to do. The common people thought him of a courteous and gentle nature, because he would not tread his enemy under his foot when he had the upper hand of him, nor be revenged of him when he had overcome him; but wise men judged it otherwise, that it was wisely done of him not to provoke Pompey.

Part Three

About this time [*actually a bit before*], Lucullus returned from the war, of the which it seemed that **Pompey had taken the honour and glory from him for the ending of it**, and was likely also to have been put from his honour of triumph, because **Gaius Memmius** was his adversary, who laid many accusations against him before the people, rather to please Pompey than for any malice else he had towards him. But Cato, both for that Lucullus was his brother-in-law, and had married his own sister Servilia, as also for that he saw they did him wrong: resisted this Memmius, thereby exposing himself to much slander and misrepresentation, insomuch that they would have turned *him* out of his office, pretending that he used his power tyrannically. Yet at length Cato so far prevailed against Memmius that he was forced to let fall the accusations, and abandon the contest. Thus Lucullus, having obtained the honour of triumph, did embrace Cato's friendship more than before, taking him for a sure **bulwark** and defense against the power of Pompey the Great.

But Pompey, shortly after returning home again, with great honour from his conquests, trusting that for respect of his welcome he should be denied nothing at the people's hands when he came home, sent before unto the Senate, to pray them for his sake to defer the election of the consuls until he came to Rome, that being present he might **favour Piso's suit, suing to be consul**. Thereunto the most part of the Senate gave their consent; but Cato on the other side was against it, not that the deferring of the time was a matter of such importance, but to cut all hope from Pompey to go about to attempt any new **devices**, insomuch that he made the Senate change opinion again, and Pompey's request was denied. Pompey being marvellously troubled withal, and perceiving that Cato would be against him in all things if he found not some device to win him: he sent for his friend **Munatius**, by his means to demand Cato's two nieces of him which were marriable: the eldest for himself, and the youngest for his son. (Others say also that they were not his nieces, but his own daughters.) Munatius proposed the matter to Cato, in presence of his wife and sisters; the women were full of joy at the prospect of an alliance with so great and important a person. But Cato making no further delay, without other deliberation, as not greatly pleased with the motion, answered him presently: "Munatius, go thy way unto Pompey again, and tell him that Cato is not to be won by women, though otherwise I mislike not of his friendship: and withal, that so long as he shall deal uprightly in all causes, and none otherwise, that he shall find him more assuredly his friend than by any alliance of marriage; and yet, that to satisfy Pompey's pleasure and will against his country, he will never give him such pledges."

The women and his friends at that time were angry with his answer and refusal, saying, it was too stately and uncourteous. But afterwards it chanced, that Pompey suing to have one of his friends made consul, **he sent a great sum of money to bribe the voices of the people**; which liberality was noted, and spoken of, because the money was counted out **in Pompey's own garden**. Then did Cato tell the women of his house that if he had now been bound by alliance of marriage unto Pompey, he should then have been driven to have been partaker of Pompey's shameful acts. When they heard what he had told them, they all confessed then that he was wiser to refuse such alliance, than they were that wished and desired it.

And yet, if men should judge of wisdom, by the success and event of things: I must needs say that Cato was in great fault for refusing of this alliance. For thereby he was the cause of Pompey's **matching** with Caesar, who, joining both their powers together, was the whole destruction of the empire of Rome: whereas peradventure it had not fallen out so, if Cato fearing Pompey's light faults, had not caused him, by increasing his power with another, to commit far greater faults. Howbeit those things were yet to come.

Furthermore, Pompey being at jar with Lucullus, touching certain ordinances which he had made in the realm of Pontus, because **both the one and the other would have their ordinances to take place**: Cato favoured Lucullus, who had open wrong. Pompey therefore seeing that he was the weaker in the senate, took part with the common people, and put forth **the law for dividing of the lands amongst the soldiers**. But Cato stoutly resisting that law again, he put it by; and made Pompey thereby in a rage to acquaint himself with Publius Clodius, the most seditious and boldest person of all the tribunes; and besides that, made alliance even at that time with Caesar, whereof Cato himself **was the only author**.

Narration and Discussion

How was Metellus' proposed law defeated?

Plutarch ends here by saying that he thinks Cato was unwise, or at least not very far-sighted, by refusing to support Pompey. Why?

For older students: For those who have read Robert Bolt's play *A Man for All Seasons:* does Cato's response to Munatius sound like something More might have said about Henry VIII?

Creative narration: Make a list of ways that Cato seemed to act against Pompey, and ways that he supported him. (You could write it from Pompey's point of view: "Reasons I think Cato likes me…Reasons I think he doesn't.") This can be continued through later lessons.

Lesson Six

Introduction

Although Julius Caesar was elected praetor for 62 B.C., the same year that Cato was tribune, he left Rome before that year was done to take on a secondary role as governor of Spain. Part of the reason was that, as governor, he would be free from having to pay off certain large debts. The governorship turned out to be a very good move for Caesar, as he successfully conquered additional tribes for Rome and gained a great deal of political support.

On his return to Rome, Caesar had a choice of rewards. The first choice was a triumphal parade for his military victories; but he chose instead the chance to run for consul. He also noticed that Pompey seemed to be needing a friend; they decided that vanquishing their mutual enemies together could be advantageous for both. Crassus was invited to join their team (he had paid off some of Caesar's debts); and Clodius ("the seditious orator") grew in influence and became tribune (breaking the rule that tribunes could not be of the noble class). Bibulus, the other consul, got the booby prize.

And as for Cato? He reluctantly agreed to take an oath of loyalty to the new regime; but even so, he was given a new job…as far out of Rome as Clodius could manage.

Vocabulary

required: demanded

by his friends: by proxy, without being there in person to declare his candidacy for consul

he spent all the whole day in his oration: This is an example of a "filibuster," the attempt to delay a vote by making prolonged speeches or excessive noise.

letting fall his triumph: choosing the election over the triumph

cozening: to obtain something by deception

importunity: annoying persistence

officers' rods: the *fasces*, bundles of rods symbolizing Roman authority

keeping his wonted pace: walking at his usual speed

left it a prey unto them…: left Rome to be dominated by those who planned to enslave it

maliced of: hated by

remit: surrender, give up

for contention's sake: to continue to make his point in the argument

supplicate him: beg his forgiveness

interpose and procure his release: let Cato go

Caesar's practice tended to this end: his actions were done for this purpose

when he had won the people's favour by such laws: The law Agraria, offering free land, was calculated to increase popular support

on the commission in the case of Ptolemy: see the note under **People**

design upon him: plot against him

restore the refugees of Byzantium: certain men of Byzantium had been exiled for crimes against the state, and Cato was to oversee their homecoming

whom Clodius pursued: because of the events around the Catiline Conspiracy

he dared not trust Canidius so far: This story is also told in the *Life of Marcus Brutus.*

People

Brutus: Marcus Junius Brutus, known for his part in the assassination of Julius Caesar in 44 B.C.; subject of Plutarch's *Marcus Brutus.* He was Cato's nephew, and (after Cato's death) his son-in-law.

Gabinius Paulus: also called Aulus Gabinius or Aulus Gabinius Paulus

Bibulus: Marcus Calpurnius Bibulus (102 B.C.-48 B.C.), Roman politician, supporter of Pompey

Ptolemy (#1): King of Cyprus from 80 B.C.-58 B.C.; the brother of Ptolemy (#2). Clodius enacted a bill to make Cyprus a Roman province, and Cato was sent to persuade Ptolemy to submit without trouble. Ptolemy refused, and committed suicide.

Ptolemy (#2): Ptolemy XII Auletes, King of Egypt. He had tried to avoid allowing Egypt to be annexed (like Cyprus) by becoming allies with Rome instead. Egyptian politics forced him to seek refuge in Rome from 58-55 B.C.

Canidius: The identity of Canidius is unknown (some think his name might have been Caninius).

Historic Occasions

60-54/53 B.C.: The First Triumvirate, made up of Caesar, Pompey, and Marcus Licinius Crassus

59 B.C.: Caesar and Bibulus were consuls

58 B.C.: Calpurnius Piso and Aulus Gabinius were consuls

58 B.C.: Cato sent to Cyprus

58 B.C.: Cicero went into exile, due to continued harassment by Clodius. Clodius then had Cicero's house torn down and a temple erected on the land.

58 B.C.: Food shortages in Rome; Pompey's success in acquiring grain increased his popularity

57 B.C.: Cicero returned to Rome and had his house rebuilt

57/56 B.C.: Death of Lucullus

On the Map

Spain: Spain, at this time, was a Roman province; it was sometimes called the Two Spains because it was divided into two parts

Gaul: a northern territory which included parts of France, Germany, and northern Italy

Illyria: the region on the eastern side of the Adriatic Sea, north of Greece and west of Macedon

Cyprus: an island country in the Mediterranean Sea, which had been conquered by Alexander the Great and then claimed by Egypt before becoming part of the Roman empire

Byzantium: now Istanbul

Isle of Rhodes: a large island southeast of Athens

Reading

Part One

Caesar, returning out of **Spain** from his praetorship, **required** the honour of triumph, and at the same time made suit to be consul. But there being a law to the contrary, that they that sued to be consuls should be present themselves *in* the city, and such also as desired honour of triumph, should be *without* the city, he earnestly required the Senate that he might sue for the consulship **by his friends**. The most part of the Senate were willing unto it, but Cato was flatly against it. He perceived that the other senators were willing to gratify Caesar: so when it came to him to deliver his opinion, **he spent all the whole day in his oration**, and by this policy prevented the senate so that they could not conclude anything. Then Caesar, **letting fall his triumph**, came into the town, and immediately made a friendship with Pompey, and stood for the consulship. As soon as he was declared consul-elect, he married his daughter Julia to Pompey. And having thus combined themselves together against the commonwealth, the one proposed laws for dividing the lands among the poor people, and the other was present to support the proposals. Lucullus, Cicero, and their friends, joined with **Bibulus**, the other consul, to hinder their passing; and, foremost of them all, Cato, who already looked upon the friendship and alliance of Pompey and Caesar as very dangerous, declared he did not so much dislike the advantage the people should get by this division of the lands, as he feared the reward these men would gain by thus courting and **cozening** the people.

Therewithal, the Senate were wholly of his opinion, and so were many other honest men of the people besides, that were not of the Senate, and who took his part: marvelling much, and also being offended with Caesar's great unreasonableness and **importunity**; who by the authority of his consulship did prefer such things as the most seditious tribunes of the people were wont commonly to do, to curry favour with the people, and by such vile means sought to make them at his commandment. Wherefore, Caesar and his friends fearing so great enemies, fell to open force. For to begin withal, as the consul Bibulus was going to the marketplace, there was a basket of dung poured upon his head: and furthermore, the **officers' rods**, which they carried before him, were broken in their hands. In fine, darts were thrown at them out of every corner, and many of them being hurt, they all at length were driven to flee, and leave the marketplace. But Cato came last of all, **keeping his wonted pace**, and he often cast back his head, and cursed such citizens.

So, they did not only pass this law Agraria by voices of the people;

but furthermore they added to it that all the Senate should be sworn to establish that law, and be bound to defend the same (if any attempted the alteration thereof), upon great penalties and fines to be set on his head, that should refuse the oath. All the other senators swore against their wills, remembering the example of the mischief that chanced unto the old Metellus, who was banished out of Italy because he would not swear to such a like law. Whereupon, the women that were in Cato's house besought him, with the tears in their eyes, that he would yield and take the oath: and so did also divers of his friends besides. Howbeit, he that most enforced and brought Cato to swear, was Cicero the orator: who persuaded him, that peradventure he would be thought unreasonable, that being but one man, he should seem to mislike that, which all other had thought meet and reasonable: and that it were a fond part of him willfully to put himself in so great danger, thinking to hinder a matter already past remedy. But yet that besides all this, a greater inconvenience would happen, if he forsook his country (for whose sake he did all these things), and **left it a prey unto them which sought the utter subversion of the same**, as if he were glad to be rid from the trouble of defending the commonwealth.

"For," said he, "though Cato have no need of Rome, yet Rome hath need of Cato, and so have all his friends": of the which, Cicero said, he was the chief, and was most **maliced of** Publius Clodius the tribune, who sought to drive him out of the country. It is said that Cato being won by these like words and persuasions at home, and openly in the marketplace, they so softened him, that he came to take his oath last of all men, except for one Favonius, a friend of his.

Caesar's heart being then lifted up, for that he had brought his first purpose to pass: he began now to prefer another law, to divide all Campania, and the country called Terra Di Lavoro ("The Land of Labour") unto the poor needy people of Rome; and no man stood against him but Cato. Whereupon Caesar made his officers to take him from the pulpit for orations, to carry him to prison. [Yet Cato did not even thus **remit** his freedom of speech, but as he went along continued to speak against the law, and advised the people to put down all legislators who proposed the like. The senate and the best of the citizens followed him with sad and dejected looks, showing their grief and indignation by their silence, so that Caesar could not be ignorant how much they were offended; but **for contention's sake** he still persisted, expecting Cato should either **supplicate him**, or make an appeal. But when he saw that he did not so much as think of doing either, ashamed of what he was doing and of what people thought of it, he himself privately bade one of the tribunes **interpose and procure his release.**

In fine, all **Caesar's practice tended to this end**: that **when he had won the people's favour by such laws**, they should then grant him the government of all the **Gauls** (as well on this side, as beyond the mountains); and all **Illyria**, with an army of four legions, for the space of five years; notwithstanding that Cato told the people before, that they themselves with their own voices did set up a tyrant that one day would cut their throats.

They did also choose Publius Clodius tribune of the people, who was of a noble house: a thing directly contrary to the law. But this Clodius had promised them, if they would help him to banish Cicero out of Rome, to do all that he could for them. Furthermore, they made Calpurnius Piso (Caesar's wife's father) and **Gabinius Paulus**, (a man wholly at Pompey's commandment, as they write which knew his life and manners) consuls the next year following.

Part Two

Now, notwithstanding that Caesar and Pompey had the rule of the commonwealth in their own hands, and that they had won part of the city with bribes, and the other part also with fear: yet they were both afraid of Cato, when they considered what trouble they had to overcome him, and remembered with vexation what pains and trouble their success over him had cost them, and indeed what shame and disgrace, when at last they were driven to use violence to him. Furthermore, Clodius utterly despaired that he could possibly banish Cicero, so long as Cato was there.

Therefore, having first laid his design, as soon as he came into his office, he sent for Cato, and told him that he looked upon him as the most incorrupt of all the Romans, and was ready to show he did so. "For whereas," said he, "many have applied to be sent to **Cyprus on the commission in the case of Ptolemy (#1)** and have solicited to have the appointment, I think you alone are deserving of it, and I desire to give you the favour of the appointment."

Cato at once cried out it was a mere **design upon him**, and no favour, but an injury. Then Clodius proudly and fiercely answered, "If you will not take it as a kindness, you shall go, though never so unwillingly"; and immediately going into the assembly of the people, he made them pass a decree that Cato should be sent to Cyprus. But they ordered him neither ship, nor soldier, nor any attendant, except two secretaries, one of whom was a thief and a rascal; and the other a retainer to Clodius. Besides, as if Cyprus and Ptolemy were not work sufficient, he was ordered also to **restore the refugees of Byzantium**. For Clodius was resolved to keep him far enough off whilst he himself continued as tribune. Cato being driven by necessity to obey, he counselled Cicero (**whom Clodius pursued**) to beware that he made no stir against him, for fear of bringing Rome into civil war and murder for his sake; but rather to absent himself, that he might another time preserve his country.

After that, he sent his friend **Canidius** before into Cyprus, unto Ptolemy (#1), to persuade him to be quiet without war: declaring unto him that he should neither lack honour nor riches, for the Romans would grant him the priesthood of Venus in the city of Paphos. Cato in the meantime remained in the **Isle of Rhodes**, preparing himself there, and abiding his answer.

Part Three

In the time of these stirs, **Ptolemy King of Egypt (#2)**, for a certain offence and discord with his subjects, departing out of Alexandria, sailed towards Rome, hoping that Caesar and Pompey with a great army would restore him to his crown and kingdom again. He being desirous to see Cato, sent unto him, supposing he would come at his sending for him. Cato by chance was occupied at that time about some business, and bade the messenger to ask Ptolemy to come to him, if he would see him. So when Ptolemy came, he neither went to meet him, nor rose up unto him, but only welcomed him, and bade him sit down. It amazed the king, at the first, to see, under so simple and mean a train, such a stateliness and majesty in Cato's behaviour. But when he heard him boldly talk with him of his affairs, and such grave talk come from him, reproving

"the folly he had committed to forsake such princely

> pleasure and wealth, to go and subject himself unto such dishonour, such extreme pains, and such passing great gifts and presents, as he should throw away to satisfy the covetousness of the rulers at Rome, the which was so insatiable, that if all the realm of Egypt were converted into silver to give among them, it would scarce suffice them: in respect whereof, he counselled him to return back with his navy, and to reconcile himself again with his subjects; offering himself also to go with him, to help to make his peace."

Then Ptolemy coming to himself, and repenting him of his folly, knowing that Cato told him truly and wisely: he determined to follow his counsel, and would have done so, had not his friends turned his mind to the contrary. So when Ptolemy came to Rome, and was driven to wait at the gates of the magistrates that were in authority: he sighed then, and repented his folly, for that he had not only despised the counsel of a wise man, but rather the oracle of a god.

Furthermore, the other Ptolemy (#1) that was in Cyprus (a happy turn for Cato) poisoned himself. Cato being also informed that he left a wonderful sum of money behind him, he determined to go himself unto Byzantium on the other business; and sent **his nephew Brutus** into Cyprus, because **he dared not trust Canidius so far**.

[*omission for length*]

Narration and Discussion

Cicero convinced Cato to take the oath of loyalty: "For," said he, "though Cato have no need of Rome, yet Rome hath need of Cato, and so have all his friends." What would you have done?

Why were Cato's warnings about Caesar ignored?

Creative narration: Dramatize one of the scenes from this passage, such as Clodius explaining to Cato why he should be happy to take on such an important job in Cyprus. Another possibility would be to interview Ptolemy (#2) after he had taken refuge in Rome.

Lesson Seven

Introduction

If Clodius had hoped that Cato would either disgrace himself or simply disappear, he was wrong. Cato returned with a certain amount of grandeur, and carrying a large amount of treasure for Rome. Although he did not accept most of the personal rewards offered to him, he did recognize that this was his chance to use the power and influence he had gained, and he decided to run for praetor.

Unfortunately, the elections that year were again marked by corruption and violence.

Vocabulary

drachma: a unit of money

extraordinary praetorship: It appears that Cato was offered the position without being elected, or possibly that he was offered an exception to the normal candidate deadlines

the authority of the consul was in Cato: Because of Cato's close connections with the consuls that year, he had as much power as if he had been consul himself.

tables: tablets recording Clodius' accomplishments as tribune

against the law: the office of tribune was supposed to be held only by non-nobles

the tribune also that did grant it him: that is, Clodius

popular: belonging to or associated with the lower classes

Pompey and Crassus having been with Caesar…: at their meeting at Lucca

prorogue: extend

Pompey's power to be joined with Crassus: if they each won one of the positions

no private person: holding a public office

came and sued: Consuls were elected late in the year and took office the first day of January; but praetors were elected separately

by the estimation of Cato: because of the great respect the people held for Cato

so wickedly given their voices: allowed themselves to be bribed

People

Philip: Lucius Marcius Philippus, consul for 56 B.C. along with **Lentulus**, a close friend of Cicero

Marcia: Cato's second wife

Lucius Domitius (Ahenobarbus): consul for 54 B.C.; an enemy of Julius Caesar; Cato's brother-in-law

Publius Vatinius: a Roman statesman who had held various offices

Historic Occasions

56 B.C.: Famous meeting of the First Triumvirate in Lucca

Early summer 56 B.C.: Probable date of Cato's return to Rome

56 B.C.: Cato divorced Marcia so that she could marry Hortensius

56 B.C.: Cicero made a speech against the acts of Clodius, but also in support of Pompey and Caesar

55 B.C.: The year began without any consuls or praetors (for complicated reasons). Pompey and Crassus were elected consuls early in the year. Cato ran for the praetorship, but was defeated by **Publius Vatinius** (who was later accused of winning by bribery).

On the Map

Tiber: the large river flowing through Rome

Reading

Part One

Having reconciled the refugees and the people of Byzantium, Cato left the city in peace and quietness; and so sailed to Cyprus, where he found a royal treasure of plate, tables, precious stones and purple, all of which was to be turned into ready money. And being determined to do everything with the greatest exactness, and to raise the price of everything to the utmost, to this end he was always present at selling the things, and went carefully into all the accounts. Nor would he trust to the usual customs of the market, but looked doubtfully upon all alike, the officers, criers, purchasers, and even his own friends; and so in fine he himself talked with the buyers, and urged them to bid high, and conducted in this manner the greatest part of the sales. This mistrustfulness offended most of his friends, and in particular, Munatius, the most intimate of them all, became almost irreconcilable.

[*omission for length: the resulting friction between Cato and his friends, though he was eventually reconciled with Munatius*]

Cato got together a little less than seven thousand talents of silver; but apprehensive of what might happen in so long a voyage by sea, he provided a great many coffers that held two talents and five hundred **drachmas** apiece; to each of these he fastened a long rope, and to the other end of the rope a piece of cork; so that if the ship should miscarry, it might be discovered whereabout the chests lay under water. Thus all the money, except a very little, was safely transported.

[*omission for length*]

Part Two

News being brought that he was come to Rome by water, when they understood that he was at hand, by and by all the magistrates, the priests, the Senate, and the most part of the people also went out to meet him by the riverside: so that both sides of the **Tiber** were full of people, and the receiving of him in, seemed not inferior to the entry of a triumph. Notwithstanding, some thought him very presumptuous that, the consuls and praetors coming out to meet him, he did not stay his galley, but rowed still up the stream (being in a king's galley of six oars to every bank); and never stayed, until all his fleet arrived in the haven. This notwithstanding, when the coffers with money were carried thorough the marketplace into the treasure chamber, the people wondered to see so great a quantity of it. And thereupon the Senate being assembled, with great and honourable words they gave Cato an **extraordinary praetorship**, and the privilege also, at any common sports, to wear a purple gown.

Cato refused all these honours; but declaring what diligence and fidelity he had found in Nicias, the steward of Ptolemy, he requested the Senate to give him his freedom.

Philip, the father of Marcia, was that year consul; so that after a sort, **the authority of the consul was in Cato**: because **Lentulus**, colleague and fellow consul with Philip, did no less reverence Cato for his virtues, than Philip did for his alliance with him.

Furthermore, when Cicero was restored again from his banishment (the which Publius Clodius, being then tribune of the people, had put upon him), and being again grown to great credit: he went one day into the Capitol, in the absence of Clodius, by force to take away the **tables** which Clodius had consecrated there, in the which were comprised all his doings during the time he was tribune. Thereupon, the Senate being assembled, Clodius did accuse Cicero of this violent fact. Cicero answered him again, that because Clodius was chosen tribune directly **against the law**, therefore all his doings were void, and of no validity. Then Cato stood up, and said he knew that all that which Clodius did when he was tribune, was scantly good and allowable; but yet if generally any man should undo all that he had passed by that authority, then all that he himself had done likewise in Cyprus, must of necessity be revoked. For the commission that was granted unto him (by virtue whereof he had done many things) should be unlawful: because **the tribune also that did grant it him**, was not lawfully chosen. And therefore, that Publius Clodius was not made tribune against the law, who by consent of the law was taken out from a noble house, and made a **popular** person; howbeit, if he had behaved himself undutifully in his office, as other men that haply had offended, then he was to be accused to make him mend his fault, and not to destroy the authority of the office(r), which in itself was lawful.

Cicero took this ill, and for a long time discontinued his friendship with Cato; but they were afterwards reconciled.

Part Three

Pompey and Crassus, having been with Caesar to talk with him (who for that purpose came out of Gaul beyond the Alps), made an agreement there betwixt them, to demand the second consulship together; and when they had it, then to **prorogue** Caesar's government for five years more; and also they would have the best provinces and greatest, for themselves, with great armies, and money enough to pay them with. This was indeed a plain conspiracy to divide the empire of Rome between them, and utterly to overthrow the state of the commonwealth.

At that time there were many noblemen which came to make suit for the consulship. But when they saw Pompey and Crassus offer to make suit for it, all the rest gave over but **Lucius Domitius** that had married Porcia, Cato's sister: through whose persuasion he would not relinquish his suit, considering that it was not the office only of the consulship that was the chiefest matter of importance, but the liberty of the Senate and people. Straight (away) there ran a rumour through the most part of the people, that they were not to suffer **Pompey's power to be joined with Crassus** by means of this office: for then his authority would be too great and strong, and therefore, that of necessity one of these two were to be denied. For these reasons the good men took part with Domitius, whom they exhorted and encouraged to go on, assuring him that many who feared openly to appear for him would privately assist him. Pompey's party, fearing this, laid wait for Domitius, and set upon him as he was going before daylight, with torches, into the Field of Mars, where the election was always made; and first striking the torchbearer that went before him, they hurt him so sore, that he fell down dead at his feet.

Then several others being wounded, all the rest fled, except Cato and Domitius, whom Cato held, though himself were wounded in the arm; and, crying out, conjured the others to stay, and not, while they had any breath, forsake the defense of their liberty against those tyrants, who plainly showed with what moderation they were likely to use the power which they endeavoured to gain by such violence.

All this notwithstanding, Domitius would tarry no longer, but betook him to his legs, and ran home. Thus were Crassus and Pompey, without denial, proclaimed consuls.

Part Four

Cato never yielded therefore, but **came and sued to be praetor**, because that thereby he might yet make it some strength and countenance to him against their consulship; that being **no private person**, he should have some better authority to resist them that were the chiefest persons. But they (Pompey and Crassus), fearing that the praetorship, **by the estimation of Cato**, would come to equal their authority of the consulship [*omission for length*]: they procured Vatinius to be chosen praetor instead of Cato. And the report went that the people that had **so wickedly given their voices**, feeling themselves pricked in conscience, fled immediately out of the field: and the honest men that remained were both very sorry and angry for the injury they had offered Cato. At that time, one of the tribunes keeping an assembly of the city, Cato stood up, and told (as if he had prophesied) before them all, what would happen to the commonwealth by these practices; and stirred up the people against Pompey and Caesar, saying that they were guilty of those things, and therefore procured them to be done, because they were afraid that if Cato had been praetor, he would too narrowly have sifted out their devices. In fine, Cato going home to his house, had more company to wait upon him alone, than all the other praetors that had been chosen.

Narration and Discussion

How did Cato turn his "punishment job" into a positive opportunity?

Cato lost the election, but he seemed to gain in other ways. Explain.

For older students: Cato responded to Cicero's speech by justifying the authority of Clodius, his enemy. Why did he do that?

Creative narration: You are friends with the owner and editor of the

Rome Daily News, who is struggling over what to write about the election events. Give some suggestions.

Lesson Eight

Introduction

The next two or three years continued to be full of power struggles and unrest. The bright spot for Cato was that he did win the praetorship for a year, although, according to Plutarch, he seemed not to care much about showing proper dignity on the judge's seat. He took charge of trying to keep that year's elections honest, which seemed to work quite well except for the fact that it made his enemies want, more than ever, to end his influence.

In 52 B.C., the threat of anarchy was serious enough for the Senate to take the emergency measure of making Pompey sole consul for that year. Unexpectedly, Cato agreed with the proposal, and it was passed.

Vocabulary

precipitate: unload

without any coat: this may refer to the praetor's robe, which Cato seems to have refused to wear

obnoxious: disagreeable

mastered the tumult: quieted everyone down

commendation: praise

constitutional acuteness: natural quickness of mind

railers: hecklers

People

Gaius Trebonius: a tribune

Historic Occasions

54 B.C.: Lucius Domitius Ahenobarbus and Claudius Pulcher were consuls; Cato was praetor

54 B.C.: Death of Pompey's wife Julia

53 B.C.: Death of Crassus in Syria

January 52 B.C.: The murder of Clodius by order of Milo

52 B.C.: Pompey chosen as sole consul (he asked Metellus Scipio to join him later in the year)

On the Map

Spain, Africa, Egypt, Syria: It would be helpful to look at a map showing these Roman provinces.

Reading

Part One

Gaius Trebonius now proposed the law for allotting provinces to the consuls, one of whom was to have **Spain** and **Africa,** the other **Egypt** and **Syria**, with full power of making war, and carrying it on both by sea and land, as they should think fit. When this was proposed, all others despaired of putting any stop to it, and neither did nor said anything against it. Then Cato getting up into the pulpit for orations, before the people began to give their voices, could hardly have two hours' space to speak: but at length, they perceiving that he delayed time by foretelling things to come, would suffer him to speak no longer, but sent a sergeant to him, and plucked him by force out of the pulpit. But when he was beneath, and cried out notwithstanding, and divers gave good ear unto him: the sergeant went to him again, and took him, and carried him out of the marketplace. Howbeit the officer had no sooner left him, but he went straight towards the pulpit for orations, crying out to the people to stand by him. When he had done this several times, Trebonius grew very angry, and commanded him to be carried to prison. The people followed him hard notwithstanding, to hear what he said unto them. Whereupon Trebonius fearing some stir, was forced to command his sergeant to let Cato go [*omission*].

The next morning notwithstanding, the contrary faction having partly put the Romans in fear, and won the other part also by fair words and money, and by force of arms likewise kept Aquilius, one of the tribunes, from coming out of the Senate; and after they had also violently driven Cato out of the marketplace, for saying that it thundered; and having hurt many men, and also slain some out of hand in the marketplace, in the end they forcibly passed the decree by voices of the people. Many being offended therewith, went a company of them together to pluck down Pompey's images; but Cato would not suffer them.

Again, another law was proposed, concerning the provinces and legions of Caesar. Upon this occasion Cato did not apply himself to the people, but appealed to Pompey himself; and told him he did not consider now that he was setting Caesar upon his own shoulders, who would shortly grow too weighty for him; and at length, not able to lay down the burden, nor yet to bear it any longer, he would **precipitate** both it and himself with it upon the commonwealth; and then he would remember Cato's advice, which was no less advantageous to him than just and honest in itself. Cato used many of these persuasions sundry times unto him, but Pompey never made account of them: for he would not be persuaded that Caesar would ever change in that sort, and besides he trusted too much to his own power and prosperity.

Furthermore, Cato was chosen praetor for the next year following, in the which it appeared (though he ministered justice uprightly) that he rather defaced and impaired the majesty and dignity of his office, than that he gave it grace and countenance by his doings: for he would oftentimes go afoot barelegged, and **without any coat**, unto his praetor's chair, and there judge matters of life and death, and upon men of great account. And some report that he would give audience right after he had dined, and drunk wine; but that is untrue.

Part Two

The people were at that time extremely corrupted by the gifts of those who sought offices, and most made a constant trade of selling their voices. Cato was eager utterly to root this corruption out of the commonwealth; he therefore persuaded the Senate to make an order that those who were chosen into any office, though nobody should accuse them, should be obliged to come into the court, and give account upon oath of their proceedings in their election. This was extremely **obnoxious** to those who stood for the offices, and yet more to those vast numbers who took the bribes. Whereupon, a great number of them went one morning to the place where he kept his audience, and all cried out upon him, reviled him, and threw stones at him. Those that were about the tribunal presently fled, and Cato himself being forced thence, and jostled about in the throng, very narrowly escaped the stones that were thrown at him, and with much difficulty got hold of the rostra; where, standing up with a bold and undaunted countenance, he at once **mastered the tumult**, and silenced the clamour; and addressing them in fit terms for the occasion, was heard with great attention, and perfectly quelled the sedition. The Senate giving him great **commendation** therefore, he told them roundly and plainly: "But I have no cause to praise you, to leave a praetor in such danger of his life, offering no aid to help him."

But the suitors for the offices, they were in a marvellous case: for one way, they were afraid to give money to buy the peoples' voices, and on the other side, they were afraid also if any other did it, that they should go without their suit. So they were all agreed together, every man, to put down one hundred and twenty-five thousand drachmas apiece; and then they should make their suit justly and uprightly: on condition that if anyone was found to make use of bribery he should forfeit the money. This agreement being concluded between them, they chose Cato (as it is reported) for their arbitrator, and keeper of all the same money. This match was made in Cato's house, where they all did put in caution or sureties to answer the money: the which he took, but would not meddle with.

The day being come, Cato assisting the tribune that governed the election, and carefully marking how they did give their voices: he spied one of the suitors for the office break the accord agreed upon, and condemned him to pay the forfeiture unto the rest. But they, greatly commending his justice and integrity, forgave the forfeiture, thinking it punishment enough unto him that had forfeited to be condemned by Cato. But thereby Cato procured himself the displeasure of the other senators, for that he seemed therein to take upon him the power and authority over the whole court, and election. For there is no virtue whereof the honour and credit doth procure more envy, than justice: because the people do commonly respect and reverence that more than any other. For they do not honour the just as they do valiant men; nor have them in admiration, as they do wise men; but they love and trust them better. As for the two first, the one they are afraid of, and the other they distrust; beside, they suppose that valiancy and wisdom come rather by the benefit of nature, than of our intent and choice; they look upon valour as a certain natural strength of the mind, and wisdom as a **constitutional acuteness**; whereas a man has it in his power to be just, if he have but the will to be so, and therefore injustice is thought the most dishonourable, because it is least excusable. This was the cause why all the noblemen in manner were against Cato, as though he only had overcome *them*.

Pompey, especially, thought that the estimation of Cato was altogether the ruin of his own power, and therefore did daily raise up many **railers** against him. One of them was Publius Clodius, that seditious tribune, who was again fallen in friendship with Pompey. He accused Cato, and cried out upon him, how he had robbed the commonwealth of a wonderful treasure, by his commission in Cyprus; and that he was enemy unto Pompey, because he did refuse to marry his daughter. Cato thereto made answer,

> "that he had brought more gold and silver, out of Cyprus, into the treasury of Rome, without the allowance of either horse or soldier, than Pompey had done with all his triumphs and wars, with the which he had troubled all the world [*omission for length*]."

Thus was he revenged of Pompey.

Part Three

[*Omission for length: the tension in Rome grew, first over an election which was cancelled due to cheating, and then because of the murder of Clodius.*]

After this, Scipio, Hypsaeus, and Milo stood to be consuls; and that not only with the usual and now recognized disorders of bribery and corruption, but with arms and slaughter, and every appearance of carrying their audacity and desperation to the length of actual civil war. Whereupon it was proposed that Pompey might be empowered to preside over that election. This Cato at first opposed, saying that the laws ought not to seek protection from Pompey, but Pompey from the laws. Yet the confusion lasting a long time, the Forum continually, as it were, besieged with three armies, and no possibility appearing of a stop being put to these disorders, Cato at length agreed that, rather than fall into the last extremity, the senate should freely confer all on Pompey; since it was necessary to make use of a lesser illegality as a remedy against the greatest of all, and better to set up a monarchy themselves than to suffer a sedition to continue that must certainly end in one.

Bibulus, Cato's friend and kinsman, made a motion to the Senate that they would choose Pompey sole consul. "For," said he, "either the commonwealth shall be well governed by him, or else Rome shall serve an ill lord." Cato then rising up, beyond all men's expectation, confirmed Bibulus' opinion, and said that the city were better to have one sovereign magistrate than none, and that he hoped Pompey could give present order for the pacifying of this confusion, and that he would be careful to preserve the city, when he saw that they trusted him with the government thereof. Thus was Pompey by Cato's means chosen sole consul.

Then he sent for Cato to come to his gardens to him, which were in the suburbs of the city. Cato went thither, and was received with as great honour and courtesy of Pompey, as could be devised: and in the end, after he had given him great thanks for the honours he had done him, he prayed him to afford him his advice and counsel in his government. Cato answered him thus, that he had not spoken anything before that time in respect of any ill will he bore him; neither that he delivered this last opinion of his in respect of his friendship; but wholly for the commonwealth's sake. In private, if he asked him, he would freely give his advice; and in public, though he asked him not, he would always speak his opinion.

[*omission for length*]

Narration and Discussion

How did Cato try to ensure honesty between the election candidates?

How was Cato "revenged of Pompey?"

Creative narration: Give Pompey's account (to someone else) of the conversation he had with Cato. You might want to add to the list of "Reasons I Think Cato Likes Me…I Think."

Lesson Nine

Introduction

Pompey had his year as consul, and afterwards seemed to believe that his position in Rome was secure, and that the Senate would continue to support his interests. He was also distracted at this time by a recent marriage. When advised that Caesar's military activities were becoming dangerous, he insisted that Caesar a) could not become *that* powerful and b) would not do anything bad.Cato ran for consul, with the goal of blocking Caesar as much as possible. However, he lost the election; and Caesar's friends pushed for even more loopholes and leeway, such as extending his command in Gaul, and even proposing that he be allowed to run for consul although he was out of the country.

In 50 B.C., Pompey became seriously ill while visiting Naples. When he was able to travel again, he was cheered and applauded in every town he passed through. This assisted his recovery, but it also increased his false sense of security. When Caesar committed his act of war, Pompey finally realized that it was time to leave town; and Cato followed behind him.

Vocabulary

the negligent security…: his careless belief about his safety

timorous: fearful

he was put from his consulship: he lost the election

Field of Mars: an open public area

nor yet by making the like suit again…: it was not worth risking another loss by running another time

premeditated discourse: prepared speech

let him have a successor: suggest that it was time for him to step down as governor

Hortensius being dead: see **Cato's Family** in the introductory notes

a mercenary design in his marriage: interested only in the money

committed: entrusted

People

Sulpicius Rufus: an orator and jurist

Germans, Britons, Gauls: various northern tribes

Historic Occasions

52 B.C.: Cato ran unsuccessfully for consul (in the election for 51 B.C.)

51 B.C.: Sulpicius Rufus and Marcus Claudius Marcellus (brother of M. Maior) were consuls

50 B.C.: Aemilius Lepidus Paullus and Gaius Claudius Marcellus (nicknamed Marcellus Minor, to distinguish him from his cousin) were consuls

50 B.C.: Hortensius died

49 B.C.: Another Gaius Claudius Marcellus (nicknamed Marcellus Maior, cousin of M. Minor) and Lentulus Crus were consuls

January 49 B.C.: Cato asked the Senate to order Caesar to disperse his army and return to Rome. Caesar insisted on keeping command of one province. Cato and Lentulus refused to back down, and this led to Caesar's act of war.

January 49 B.C.: Caesar crossed the Rubicon

49 B.C.: Marcia and her children returned to Cato's house

On the Map

Ariminium: now Rimini; a city in northern Italy. Caesar's capture of the town, after he crossed the Rubicon, was an act of open rebellion.

Bruttium: the Italian region of Calabria

Reading

Part One

Things proceeding in this sort at Rome, Caesar remained in Gaul with his army, where he made wars; nevertheless he won himself friends still in Rome, by gifts and money, and made himself very strong. And now Cato's old admonitions began to rouse Pompey out of **the negligent security in which he lay**, into a sort of imagination of danger at hand; but seeing him slow and unwilling, and **timorous** to undertake any measures of prevention against Caesar, Cato resolved himself to stand for the consulship, and presently force Caesar either to lay down his arms or reveal his intentions. Both Cato's competitors were persons of good position: **Sulpicius**, who was one, owed much to Cato's credit and authority in the city, and it was thought unhandsome, and ungratefully done, to stand against him; not that Cato himself took it ill, "For it is no wonder," said he, "if a man will not yield to another in that which he esteems the greatest good."

This notwithstanding he persuaded the Senate to make a law that, from thenceforth, such as sued for any office should themselves ask the people for their votes, and not prefer their suit by others. This caused the people to be more offended with him than before, because thereby he did not only take away their fingering of money, which they got by their voices in elections; but took from them the means they had also to pleasure many, bringing them now into poverty and contempt. He therefore having no face to flatter the people and to curry favor with them, but rather sticking to his grave manner and modest life, than to seek the dignity of a consul by such means: made suit himself in person, and would not suffer his friends to take the ordinary course which might win the people's hearts, whereupon **he was put from his consulship**. This denial was wont not only to have made the parties refused very sorrowful, but their friends and kinsmen also greatly ashamed a long time after. Howbeit Cato made no reckoning of that, but went the next morning, and played at tennis with his friends in the **Field of Mars**; and, after he had dined, he walked again in the marketplace, as his manner was, without shoes on his feet, or coat. But Cicero blamed him much for that, because the commonwealth requiring then such a consul as he, he had not carefully endeavoured himself by courtesy and gentle means to win the favour of the people, neither would ever after make suit for it, although at another time he sued to be praetor. Thereunto Cato answered, that for the praetorship, he was not denied it by the goodwill of the people, but rather for that they were bribed with money. And for the election of the consuls, where there was no deceit used, he knew plainly he went without it because of his manners which the people misliked: the which he thought were no wise man's part to change for any man's pleasure; **nor yet by making the like suit again, to hazard the refusal**.

Part Two

Furthermore, Caesar making war with very stout nations, and having with no small danger and travail subdued them; and having also set upon the **Germans**, with whom the Romans were at peace, and also slain three hundred thousand persons: his friends made suit that the people should do solemn sacrifice to give thanks unto the gods. But Cato, in open Senate, was of opinion that they should deliver Caesar into their hands, whom he had injured, to receive such punishment as they thought good: to the end the whole offence, for the breach of peace, might be cast upon him, that the city might be no partaker of it, since they could not do withal. "Nevertheless," said he, "we are to do sacrifices unto the gods, to give them thanks, for that they turned not the revenge for the fury and rashness of the captain upon our poor soldiers which were in no fault, but have pardoned the commonwealth."

Caesar being advertised thereof, wrote a letter unto the Senate, containing many accusations against Cato. The letter being read, Cato rose, [and seemed not at all concerned; and without any heat or passion, but in a calm and, as it were, **premeditated discourse**, made all Caesar's charges against show like mere common scolding and abuse, and in fact a sort of pleasantry and play on Caesar's part; and proceeding then to go into all Caesar's political courses, and to explain and reveal (as though he had been not his constant opponent, but his fellow-conspirator) his whole conduct and purpose from its commencement, he concluded by telling the senate, it was not the sons of the **Britons** or the **Gauls** they need fear, but Caesar himself, if they were wise. He thereupon so offended the Senate, and made such stir among them, that Caesar's friends repented them they had caused his letters to be read in the Senate, giving Cato thereby occasion justly to complain of Caesar, and to allege much good matter against him.

At that time therefore there was nothing decreed in the Senate against Caesar, but this was said only, that it were good reason to **let him have a successor**. Then Caesar's friends made suit that Pompey as well should put away his army, and resign up the provinces he kept, or else that they should compel Caesar no more than him to do it. Then Cato opened his mouth, and said that the thing was now come to pass which he had ever told them of, and that Caesar came to oppress the commonwealth, openly turning the army against it, which deceitfully he had obtained of the same.

All this prevailed not, neither could he thereby win anything of the Senate, because the people favoured Caesar, and would always have him great: for the Senate did believe all that he said, but for all that they feared the people. But when the news was brought that Caesar had seized Ariminium, and was marching with his army toward Rome, then all men, even Pompey, and the common people too, cast their eyes on Cato, who had alone foreseen and first clearly declared Caesar's intentions.

Then said Cato unto them: "If you would have believed me, my lords, and followed my counsel, you should not now have been afraid of one man alone, neither should you also have put your only hope in one man." Pompey answered thereunto that Cato indeed had guessed more truly, howbeit that he also had dealt more friendly. Thereupon Cato gave counsel that the Senate should refer all unto Pompey's order:

"For," said he, "they that can do great mischief, know also how to help it."

Part Three

Pompey, finding he had not sufficient forces, and that those he could raise were not very resolute, forsook the city. Cato, resolving to follow Pompey into exile, sent his younger son to Munatius, who was then in the country of **Bruttium**, and took his eldest son with him; but wanting somebody to keep his house and take care of his daughters, he took Marcia again, who was now a rich widow, **Hortensius being dead**, and having left her all his estate. Caesar afterward made use of this action also to reproach him with covetousness, and **a mercenary design in his marriage**.

[*omission for length*]

As soon, however, as he had again taken Marcia, he **committed** his house and his daughters to her, and himself followed Pompey. And it is said, that from that day he never cut his hair, nor shaved his beard, nor wore a garland; but was always full of sadness, grief, and dejectedness for the calamities of his country; and continually showed the same feeling to the last, whatever party had misfortune or success.

Narration and Discussion

In Part One, why was Cicero so annoyed with Cato's (mis)handling of the election campaign?

Some of the senators praised the gods when they heard of the slaughter among the northern tribes. What was Cato's response?

For older students: Discuss this statement: "Thereupon Cato gave counsel that the Senate should refer all unto Pompey's order: 'For,' said he, 'they that can do great mischief, know also how to help it.'"

Creative narration: "Pompey, finding he had not sufficient forces, and that those he could raise were not very resolute, forsook the city…

On a first reading, those words might not carry much meaning; but the Republic had just turned upside-down. Imagine that you are a Roman trying to explain recent events to a visitor. What would you say?

Lesson Ten

Introduction

The last three lessons take place against the backdrop of Julius Caesar's overthrow of the Roman government. After illegally crossing the Rubicon River with his army, Caesar was declared an enemy of the state. Pompey, along with other senators, left Rome to gather and train an army in Greece. As a supporter of Pompey, Cato was sent to the colony of Syracuse, on the island of Sicily, to secure the grain supply for the army. However, his troops were overcome by **Curio's** forces; so Cato then went to Greece to join Pompey.

For reasons of length, the above events, plus the battles of Dyrrhachium and Pharsalus, are **not included here**. (Older students may wish to read Plutarch's full text.) However, even after Pompey's defeat and death, many of the Roman loyalists continued to fight against Caesar's domination. These included Cato and Metellus Scipio, who both escaped to Africa and led resistance from the city of Utica. We rejoin the story at that point.

Vocabulary

sit at table: As mentioned in the previous lesson, Cato was refusing the comfort of "reclining" or lying down at dinner, as a sign of his grief over what had happened to Rome

proconsul: governor of a province, with authority similar to that of a consul within that jurisdiction. A **propraetor (Dryden: proprietor)** is someone acting with the authority of a praetor.

to see a Scipio command in Africa: previous members of his family were military heroes, such as Scipio Africanus (236/5 B.C.-183 B.C.)

take time: delay as much as possible; try to outlast Caesar rather than have to do battle with him

three hundred men: These were Roman business people (such as merchants and financiers) living in or visiting Utica

munition: military equipment

commend: praise

thitherunto: up to that point

tarry him: wait for him

promontory: outcropping of land

lord and emperor: This is a figure of speech; Rome did not yet have emperors

People

(Titus) Labienus: known for his long military career

Scipio: Quintus Caecilius Metellus Pius Scipio Nasica, often called Metellus Scipio (c. 100/98 BC – 46 BC). Military commander; consul with Pompey (his son-in-law) in 52 B.C.

Juba: Juba I of Numidia

(Publius) Attius Varus: He had been praetor (governor) of the province of Africa under Pompey, and returned at this time to reclaim his province; he fought off troops led by **Curio** in 49 B.C.

Curio: Gaius Scribonius Curio is not named in Plutarch's text, except for a quick reference in **Lesson Three**. However, he is important to this part of the story, as Caesar sent him to lead his forces in Sicily and then in Africa, as described here.

Historic Occasions

April 49 B.C.: Cato left Syracuse (in Sicily) to join Pompey

48 B.C.: Battle of Dyrrhachium; Battle of Pharsalus

48 B.C.: Death of Bibulus

48 B.C.: Death of Pompey

December 47 B.C.: Caesar's troops landed in Africa

April 46 B.C.: Caesar defeated loyalist forces at Thapsus

On the Map

Cyrene: a city in what is now Libya

Utica: a city in what is now Tunisia, founded by the Phoenicians but taken by the Romans in the Third Punic War

Thapsus: a port city in what is now Tunisia

Reading

Prologue

Leading troops he had gathered on his journey, Cato marched against the city of **Cyrene**, which presently received him, though not long before they had shut their gates against **Labienus**. Here he was informed that **Scipio**, Pompey's father-in-law, was received by **King Juba**; and that **Attius Varus**, whom Pompey had made governor of the province of **Africa**, had joined them with his forces. Cato therefore resolved to march toward them by land, it being now winter [*omission*]. They marched seven days together, Cato all the time going on foot at the head of his men, and never making use of any horse or chariot. Ever since the Battle of Pharsalus, he used to **sit at table**, and added this to his other ways of mourning, that he never lay down but to sleep.

Having passed the winter in Africa, Cato drew out his army, which amounted to little less than ten thousand. The affairs of Scipio and Varus went very ill, by reason of their dissensions and quarrels among themselves, and their submissions and flatteries to King Juba [*omission*]. However, he now succeeded both in humbling the pride of Juba, who was treating Scipio and Varus much like a pair of **satraps** under his orders, and also in reconciling them to each other. All the troops desired him to be their leader; Scipio, likewise; and Varus gave way to it, and offered him the command; but he said he would not break those laws which he sought to defend; and he, being but **propraetor**, ought not to command in the presence of a **proconsul** (for Scipio had been created proconsul); besides that, people took it as a good omen **to see a Scipio command in Africa**, and the very name inspired the soldiers with hopes of success.

Part One

Scipio, having taken upon himself the command, presently resolved, at the instigation of Juba, to put all the inhabitants of **Utica** to the sword, and to destroy the city for having, as they professed, taken part with Caesar. Howbeit Cato would not suffer him, but protesting unto them that were present, and calling the gods to witness in open council, with great difficulty he saved the poor people of Utica from that cruel tragedy and slaughter. And afterwards, upon the entreaty of the inhabitants, at the instance of Scipio, Cato took upon himself the government of Utica, lest, one way or the other, it should fall into Caesar's hands; for it was a strong place, and very advantageous for either party. Cato did both furnish it, and also fortify it. For he brought in great store of corn; he repaired the ramparts of the walls, made great high towers, and cast deep trenches round about the city, paling them in; and betwixt the trenches and the town, he lodged all the young men of Utica, and compelled them to deliver up their armour and weapons; and kept all the rest within the city itself, carefully providing, that never a man of them should be hurt by the Romans; and besides, did also send corn, armour, munition and money unto the camp: so that the city of Utica was the staple and storehouse of the wars.

Moreover, as he had before counselled Pompey not to come to battle, the like counsel he now gave also unto Scipio: not to hazard battle against a man of great skill and experience in wars, but to **take time**, whereby, by little and little, he should consume the power and strength of Caesar's tyranny. But Scipio out of pride rejected this counsel, and wrote a letter to Cato in which he reproached him with cowardice; and that he could not be content to lie secure himself within walls and trenches, but he must hinder others from boldly using their own good sense to seize the right opportunity. Cato wrote again unto him, that he was ready to go into Italy, with his footmen and horsemen which he had brought into Africa, to draw Caesar from them, and to turn him against him. Scipio made but a sport at it. Then Cato openly let it be seen that he was sorry he had yielded the command to Scipio, who he saw would not carry on the war with any wisdom; and if, contrary to all appearance, he should succeed, he would use his success as unjustly at home. Then he began to mistrust the good success of this war (and so he told his friends) for the general's hastiness and unskillfulness: and yet if beyond expectation it fell out well, and that Caesar were overthrown, he would never dwell at Rome anymore, but would flee the cruelty and bitterness of Scipio, who even at that present time did proudly threaten many.

Part Two

But in the end, that fell out sooner than looked for. Late in the evening came one from the army, whence he had been three days coming, who brought word there had been a great battle near **Thapsus**; that all was utterly lost; Caesar had taken the camps, Scipio and Juba were fled with a few only, and all the rest of the army was lost. This news, arriving in time of war, and in the night, so alarmed the people, that they were almost out of their wits, and could scarce keep themselves within the walls of the city. But Cato came forward, and meeting the people in this hurry and clamour, did all he could to comfort and encourage them, and somewhat appeased the fear and amazement they were in, telling them that very likely things were not so bad in truth, but much exaggerated in the report. And so he pacified the tumult for the present.

The next morning, by break of day, he made proclamation that the **three hundred men** which he had chosen for his councillors should come and assemble in the Temple of Jupiter, they all being citizens of Rome who were in Africa for business reasons; and all the Roman senators and their children also. Now whilst they gathered themselves together, Cato himself went very gravely with a set modest countenance, as if no such matter had happened, having a little book in his hand, which he read as he went. This book contained the store and preparation of **munition** he had made for this war, as corn, armour, weapons, bows, slings and footmen.

When they were all assembled, he began greatly to **commend** the good love and faithfulness of these three hundred Romans, which had profitably served their country with their persons, money, and counsel; and did counsel them not to depart one from another, as men having no hope, or otherwise seeking to save themselves scatteringly. For remaining together, Caesar would less despise them, if they would make war against him; and would also sooner pardon them, if they craved mercy of him. Therefore he counselled them

> to determine what they would do; and for his own part (he said) he would not mislike whatsoever they determined of: for if their minds followed their fortune, he would think this change to proceed of the necessity of time. But if they were resolved to withstand their misfortune, and to hazard themselves to defend their liberty: he then would not only commend them, but having their noble courage in admiration, would himself be their chieftain and companion, even to prove the fortune of their country to the uttermost. The which was not Utica, nor Adrumetum, but the city itself of Rome: the which oftentimes through her greatness, had raised herself from greater dangers and calamities [*omission for length*]. Notwithstanding, they were to think of the matter among themselves, and to make their prayers to the gods, that in recompense of their virtue and good service which they had showed **thitherunto**, they would grant them grace to determine for the best.

After Cato had ended his oration, there were divers of them that were stirred up by his lively persuasions, but the most part of them were encouraged by his constancy and noble mind, and also by his kindness: so that they presently forgot the danger they were in, and prayed him to command their persons, goods, and weapons, as he thought good, taking him for their only invincible captain, of whom fortune had no power, thinking it better to die obeying his counsel, than to save themselves, forsaking so valiant and worthy a man. Then, when one of the assembly made a motion that they should make their bondmen free, and that divers also did confirm it, Cato said he would by no means suffer it, because it was neither meet nor lawful: howbeit if their masters would set them free, that he was contented to receive them for soldiers, that could wear any weapon. Divers promised him to do it: and Cato commanded their names should be enrolled that would, and so went his way.

Part Three

Immediately after, letters were brought him from King Juba and Scipio: of the which, King Juba was hidden in a mountain with few men with him, who sent unto him to know what he would determine to do. For if he meant to forsake Utica, he would **tarry him** there: and if otherwise he determined to keep Utica, than that he would come and help him with an army. Scipio was on shipboard, near a certain **promontory**, not far from Utica, expecting an answer upon the same account. Then Cato thought it best to stay the messengers which had brought him their letters, till he saw what was the determination of the three hundred. As for the senators that were there, they showed great forwardness, and at once set free their slaves, and furnished them with arms. But the three hundred being men occupied in merchandise and money-lending, much of their substance also consisting in slaves, the enthusiasm that Cato's speech had raised in them did not long continue. As there are substances that easily admit heat, and as suddenly lose it when the fire is removed, so these men were heated and inflamed while Cato was present; but when they began to reason among themselves, the fear they had of Caesar soon overcame their reverence for Cato and for virtue.

> "For," said they, "what are we, and what is he whom we disdain to obey? Is it not Caesar himself, who at this day is **lord and emperor** of Rome? Never a one of us is Scipio, Pompey, nor Cato: and yet now, when all men for fear (and in manner compelled) do yield and submit themselves, we will needs take upon us within the walls of Utica to fight for the liberty of Rome against him for whom Cato, fleeing with Pompey, forsook Italy; and we now make our bondmen free to fight with Caesar, having no better liberty ourselves than it pleaseth him to give us. Let

> us therefore now know ourselves whilst we have time, and crave mercy at his hands that is the stronger, and send unto him, to pray him to pardon us."

The greatest and wisest men of those three hundred merchants had this speech. But the most part of them sought means how to entrap the senators, hoping the better of mercy at Caesar's hand, if they did deliver them unto him. Cato did notice this change in them, but yet uttered not that which he thought, and returned the messengers back again unto King Juba and Scipio, and wrote unto them that they should beware they came not near Utica, because he did mistrust these three hundred merchants.

Narration and Discussion

Cato kept a list of the army's equipment, food supplies and so on. What other strengths did Cato's side have? What were its weaknesses?

Throughout Cato's life, he had often seen laws (such as a **propraetor** submitting himself to a **proconsul**) pushed aside by those with ambitions to rule. To show his own respect for those laws, he placed himself under Scipio's authority; but later on, he seemed to regret his decision. Should he have broken the law and taken command himself?

Creative narration: After hearing the news of the Battle of Thapsus, Cato made a speech to the senators and merchants in Utica, encouraging them to fight for Rome, and to free their slaves so that they could fight as well. At first many of them agreed, but later they became afraid and changed their minds. Write a scene involving those becoming less convinced of their chances against Caesar.

Lesson Eleven

Introduction

Although all seemed lost, Cato remained in charge. The merchants and senators seemed to be more of a hindrance than a help, but he did have the assistance of a number of "horsemen" (cavalry officers) who had escaped from the Battle of Thapsus.

Vocabulary

tarrying: waiting

Carthaginian: Phoenician

dissembling: concealing their opinions

retaining: restraining, locking up

citadel: fort

perfidious: deceitful, untrustworthy

manifestly: obviously

vanquished: conquered

wrack: destruction

last cast: last effort (referring to the last cast or throw of the dice)

spoil and plunder: rob of treasure

dispatching the business of any that applied to him: dealing with everyone else's problems

recommended his son…: asked him to look out for them

People

Marcus Rubrius: We heard in **Lesson Two** about **Rubrius** who was propraetor in Macedon, but they were not necessarily the same person.

Marcus Octavius: this may have been an ancestor of Gaius Octavius (later Caesar Augustus)

Statilius: Also no further information. (But watch for him again in the next lesson.) Statilius also appears in Plutarch's *Marcus Brutus*.

Apollinides, Demetrius: Plutarch seems to be the only source of information on these philosophers.

Lucius Julius Caesar: a former consul; cousin of Julius Caesar, but a supporter of Pompey. He was pardoned after the Battle of Thapsus, but was killed soon afterwards, probably by Caesar's soldiers.

Reading

Part One

Now there were a great number of horsemen which had escaped from the recent battle; who, coming towards Utica, sent three of their company unto Cato; who yet did not all bring the same message; for one party was for going to Juba, another for joining with Cato, and some again were afraid to go into Utica. When Cato heard this, he ordered **Marcus Rubrius** to attend upon the three hundred, and quietly take the names of those who, of their own accord, set their slaves at liberty, but by no means to force anybody. Then taking with him the senators, he went out of the town, and met the principal officers of these horsemen, whom he entreated not to abandon so many Roman senators, not to prefer Juba for their commander before Cato, but consult the common safety, and to come into the city, which was impregnable, and well furnished with corn and other provision, sufficient for many years. The senators likewise with tears besought them to stay.

Thereupon the captains went and spoke with their soldiers. Cato in the meantime sat him down on a little hill, with the senators, **tarrying** for answer.

But then on the sudden came Rubrius unto him in great haste, complaining of the tumult of these three hundred merchants, which went about to make the city to rebel: whereupon the senators, their hearts failing them, fell to bewail their miserable fortune. But Cato sought to comfort them, and then sent unto the three hundred merchants, to pray them to have a little patience. So the captains returned again with unreasonable demands of the horsemen. For they said that they cared not for King Juba's pay, neither were they afraid of Caesar's malice, as long as they had Cato for their general; but they dreaded to be shut up with the Uticans, men of traitorous temper and **Carthaginian** blood. "For," said they, "though now they stir not, and be quiet: yet when Caesar comes, they will be the first that will betray us, and cut our throats." And therefore they said that if Cato would have them to join with him in this war, that he should either kill or drive away all the Uticans out of the city; and then that they would come into it, when it was clear of all those barbarous people, their enemies. Cato thought this a cruel and barbarous condition; nevertheless he told them that he would talk with the three hundred.

Part Two

Then he returned to the city, where he found the men, not framing excuses, or **dissembling** out of reverence to him, but openly declaring that no one should compel them to make war against Caesar; which, they said, they were neither able nor willing to do. And some there were who muttered words about **retaining** the senators till Caesar's coming; but Cato seemed not to hear this, as indeed he had the excuse of being a little deaf. At that very instant one came to him, and told him that the horsemen were going their way. Cato therefore fearing lest these three hundred merchants would lay hands upon the senators, he went unto them himself with his friends; and perceiving they were gone a great way off, he took his horse and rode after them. They, rejoicing to see him come, received him among them, and prayed him to save himself with them. But Cato prayed them again to save the senators, and that with such affection, as it forced tears in him, besides, he held up his hands unto them, took their horses by the bridles, and themselves by their weapons, till in fine he prevailed with them out of compassion to stay only that one day, to procure a safe retreat for the senators. Having thus persuaded them to go along with him, some he placed at the gates of the town, and to others gave the charge of the **citadel**. The three hundred began to fear they should suffer for their inconstancy; and sent to Cato, entreating him by all means to come to them; but the senators, flocking about him, would not suffer him to go, and said they would not trust their guardian and saviour to the hands of **perfidious** traitors.

For there had never, perhaps, been a time when Cato's virtue appeared more **manifestly**; and every class of men in Utica could clearly say, with sorrow and admiration, how entirely free was everything that he was doing from any secret motives or any mixture of self-regard; he, namely, who had long before resolved on his own death, was taking such extreme pains, toil, and care, only for the sake of others, that when he had secured their lives, he might put an end to his own. For it was easily perceived that he had determined to die, though he did not let it appear.

Part Three

Whereupon, having pacified the senators, he yielded unto the requests of the three hundred merchants, and went himself alone unto them. Then they thanked him much for his coming, and prayed him to command them, and boldly to trust them: so that he would pardon them if they could not be all "Catos," and would take pity of their faint hearts, though they were not so constant and noble-minded as he. They told him they were determined to send unto Caesar, specially to entreat him for Cato; and if that they could not obtain pardon for him, then they were assured they could have none for themselves, and therefore would fight for the safety of him, while they had any breath in their bodies.

Cato commended their good intentions, and advised them to send speedily, for their own safety; but by no means to ask anything in his behalf: for those who are conquered, entreat; and those who have done wrong, beg pardon. For himself he did not confess to any defeat in all his life, but rather, so far as he had thought fit, he had got the victory, and had conquered Caesar in all points of justice and honesty. It was Caesar that ought to be looked upon as one surprised and **vanquished**; for he was now convicted and found guilty of those designs against his country which he had so long practised and so constantly denied.

Part Four

When he had thus spoken, he went out of the assembly, and being informed that Caesar was coming with his whole army: "Ah," said he, "he expects to find us brave men." Then turning unto the senators, he gave them counsel quickly to save themselves, whilst the horsemen were yet in the city. So shutting all the gates of the city, saving that towards the harbour: he appointed ships for them all, and set everything at a stay, without tumult or disorder, no man having injury offered him, and gave every one of them money to make way for their safety.

Marcus Octavius, who came with two legions, and camped hard by Utica, sent unto Cato to determine which of them two should be general. He made no answer, but turning to his friends said: "How can we wonder any more that all goeth to **wrack** with us, since there is such ambition amongst us for the government, even now, when we are at the **last cast**?" In the meantime, word was brought him that the horse soldiers were going away, and were beginning to **spoil and plunder** the citizens. He straight ran thither himself, and the first he met withal, he took from them that which they had gotten. The rest, before he came unto them, threw down that which they were carrying away, and hanging down their heads for shame, they went their way, and said nothing. Then he called together all the people of Utica, and requested them, upon the behalf of the three hundred, not to exasperate Caesar against them, but all to seek their common safety together with them.

Then he went again to the pier, and there embracing his friends, and taking his leave of them all, he brought them to their ships. Now for his son, he did not counsel him to go, neither did he think it meet to urge him to forsake his father. Furthermore, there was one **Statilius**, a young man in his company, of a noble courage, that was determined to follow the invincible constancy of Cato: who counselled him to take the sea, and to sail away with the rest, because he knew he was Caesar's mortal enemy. Statilius said he would not go. Then Cato turning him unto **Apollonides**, a Stoic philosopher, and unto **Demetrius**, a Peripatetic philosopher, said, "It belongs to you to cool the fever of this young man's spirit, and to make him know what is good for him." And thus, in setting his friends upon their way, and in **dispatching the business of any that applied to him**, he spent that night and the greatest part of the next day.

Then **Lucius Caesar**, the kinsman of Julius Caesar the conqueror, being chosen by the three hundred to go and make suit unto him for them all, came and prayed Cato to help him to make his oration, which he should say unto Caesar for them all. "And as for thee, Cato," said he, "I will kiss his hands, and fall down on my knees before him to entreat him for thee."

"Nay," said Cato, "thou shalt not do so. For if I would save my life by Caesar's grace, I could do it, if I would but go unto him; howbeit I will not be bound to a tyrant for injustice. For it is an injustice in him to take upon him, as a lord and sovereign, to save a man's life, when himself hath no authority to command. But yet let us consider, if thou wilt, what thou shalt say to crave pardon for the three hundred." So they were a while together considering the matter, and in fine, Lucius Caesar being ready to depart, Cato **recommended his son and friends unto him**; and taking him by the hand, bade him farewell.

Narration and Discussion

How did Cato show concern for others at this time? (A Bible verse to look up: Mark 9:35)

Give your impressions of Statilius.

For older students: The Stoic philosophers lived by principles such as "A life led according to rational nature is virtuous," and "From wisdom spring insight, bravery, self-control, and justice." How did Cato's conduct during this time reflect these beliefs?

Lesson Twelve

Introduction

Seeing no possible good outcome from the war, Cato decided to take his own life. However, the events of his final night might have been written as a "black comedy," as the honourable farewell he had planned turned into a mess.

Vocabulary

sat at his meat: see previous lessons

Paradoxes: A paradox is a seemingly absurd or self-contradictory statement. The Paradoxes referred to here were the principles of Stoic philosophy. An interesting side note is that Cicero, that same year, wrote *Paradoxa Stoicorum*, a book examining those statements. In his introduction, he praises Cato without mentioning his death (i.e. it must have been written before this dinner conversation); so the then-brand-new book may have been exactly what they were discussing.

suspect the execution of his determination: suspect what he intended to do

deranged: mad, out of one's senses

dispatch: kill

envy: This has also been translated "begrudge"

Historic Occasions

April 46 B.C.: Death of Cato

46 B.C.: Suicides of King Juba and Metellus Scipio

45 B.C.: Battle of Munda ended Caesar's civil war; death of Varus

45 B.C.: Marriage of Marcus Brutus and Porcia (Cato's daughter)

September 45 B.C.: Caesar's return to Italy

March 44 B.C.: Caesar assassinated

43 B.C.: Murder of Cicero

42 B.C.: Battle of Philippi; deaths of Marcus Brutus, Statilius, and Marcus Porcius Cato (Cato's son)

Reading

Part One

Cato returned unto his lodging, and calling his son and friends before him, and talking of many matters: among others he charged his son in no case to meddle in the affairs of the commonwealth. "For," said he, "to deal uprightly like Cato's son, the corruption of the time and state will not abide it; and contrarily, observing the time, thou canst not do like an honest man."

Toward evening he went into his bath. As he was bathing, he remembered Statilius, and called out aloud, "Apollonides, have you tamed the high spirit of Statilius, and is he gone without bidding us farewell?" "No," said Apollonides, "I have said much to him, but to little purpose; he is still resolute and unalterable, and declares he is determined to follow your example." At this, it is said, Cato smiled, and answered, "That will soon be tried."

After he had bathed, he went to supper, and **sat at his meat**, as he had always used to after the Battle of Pharsalus, and never lay down but when he went to bed. There supped with him all his own friends and the magistrates of Utica. After supper, they fell into grave talk and matters of philosophy, till at length they came unto the strange **Paradoxes** of the Stoic philosophers, particularly this: that only the good man is free, and all the evil be slaves. The Peripatetic philosopher that was present there was straight against it. But Cato was very earnest against the Peripatetic, and argued the matter a long time, with a vehement speech and contention: insomuch as they that heard him, found then that he was determined to end his life and set himself at liberty.

But then when he had ended his argument, and saw that every man held his peace, and looked sadly of it: to comfort them again, and to put the suspicion of his death out of their heads: he began again to fall in talk of their affairs, showing great concern for those that were at sea, as also for the others, who, travelling by land, were to pass through a dry and barbarous desert.

Part Two

Now when supper was done, and the strangers gone, he walked, as his manner was, with his friends; and having taken order with the captains of the watch for matters of service, as the time required, then going into his chamber he embraced his son and his friends more lovingly than he was wont to do, whereby he made them again **suspect the execution of his determination**.

When he was come into his chamber and laid in his bed, he took Plato's *Dialogues* in his hand, treating of the soul, and read the most part of it. Then looking by his bedside, and missing his sword (which his son had taken from him when he was at supper), he called one of the grooms of his chamber to him, and asked him who had taken his sword away. His man made him no answer, and he fell again to read his book. A little after, not seeming importunate, or hasty for it, but as if he would only know what had become of it, he bade it be brought. But having waited some time, when he had read through the book, and still nobody brought the sword, he called up all his servants, and in a louder tone demanded his sword. To one of them he gave such a blow in the mouth, that he hurt his own hand; and now grew more angry, exclaiming that he was betrayed and delivered naked to the enemy by his son and his servants.

Then his son and friends ran unto him, and falling down on their knees, lamented, and besought him to be contented. Cato then rising out of his bed, looked grimly upon them, and said unto them:

> "When," said he, "and how did I become **deranged**, and out of my senses, that thus no one tries to persuade me by reason; or show me what is better, if I am supposed to be ill-advised? Must I be disarmed, and hindered from using my own reason? And you, young man, why do you not bind your father's hands behind him that, when Caesar comes, he may find me unable to defend myself? To **dispatch** myself I want no sword; I need but hold my breath awhile, or strike my head against the wall."

When he had said thus, his son went out of his chamber weeping, and all his friends also, no man remaining with Cato, but Demetrius and Apollonides, unto whom he spoke more gently, and reasoned in this sort:

> "What, do you think to keep an old man as I am alive by force? And have you tarried behind but to sit staring upon me, and say nothing unto me? If otherwise else, by reason you come to persuade me, that it shall be no shame for Cato, despairing of the safety of his life, to seek it by the grace and mercy of

> his enemy: why then do you not now tell me your reasons to persuade me, that forsaking all other fancies and determinations which hitherto we have held for good, having suddenly become wiser by Caesar's means, we should be bound the more therefore to give him thanks? I do not tell you this that I have determined anything of my life, but that it is in my power (if I list) to put the thing in execution I have determined: but yet I will consult with you, when I am so determined, to hear the reasons and opinion of your books, which yourselves do use in discourse and argument together. Go your way therefore hardily unto my son, and tell him that he must not think to compel his father unto that which he cannot prove good unto him by reason."

After this talk, Demetrius and Apollonides being nothing comforted, weeping, departed out of his chamber. Then his sword was brought him by a little boy. When he had it, he drew it out, and looked whether the point and edge of his sword was sharp and would cut. When he saw the point was good, "Now," said he, "I am master of myself"; and laying down the sword, he took his book again, which, it is related, he read twice over. After this he slept so soundly that he was heard to snore by those that were without.

About midnight, he called for two of his freemen, Cleanthes, his physician, and Butas, whom he chiefly employed in public business. Butas he sent unto the haven to see if all his men that were embarked were under sail: and he gave his hand unto the physician to be bound up, because it was swollen with the blow he gave one of his slaves when he hit him on the face. All his servants were glad to hear of that, hoping then that he desired to live.

Soon after came Butas back again from the haven, and brought him word that all were gone but Crassus, who stayed about some business he had, and yet that he was going to take ship: howbeit that the sea was very rough, and wind exceeding great. Cato hearing this, sighed, being sorry for them that were upon the sea; and sent Butas back again to the harbour, to see if any man came back for any matter they had to say unto him. The little birds began to chirp, and Cato fell again in a little slumber. But thereupon Butas returned, and brought him word that all was quiet in the harbour, and there was no stir. Then Cato bade him go his way, and shut the door after him, and laid him down in his bed, as though he had meant to have slept out all the rest of the night.

[*Cato then killed himself with his sword. Plutarch describes this quite graphically.*]

Part Three

Whereupon the three hundred Romans (in less time than a man would have thought Cato's own household servants could have known of his death) were at his doors; and immediately after, all the people of Utica also came thither, and with one voice called Cato their benefactor and saviour, and said he only was a free man, and had an invincible mind; and this was done when they heard that Caesar was not far from Utica.

Furthermore, neither fear of the present danger, nor the desire to flatter the conqueror, neither any private quarrel amongst themselves, could keep them from honouring Cato's funerals. For, sumptuously setting out his body, and honourably accompanying his funerals as might be, they buried him by the seaside, where at this present time is to be seen his image, holding a sword in his hand.

After that, they made their best way to save themselves and their city.

Now Caesar being advertised, by them that came unto him, how Cato stirred not from Utica, nor fled not, but sent all others away, saving himself, and his son, and a few of his friends that remained there, being afraid of nothing: he could not devise what he meant by it. Therefore esteeming Cato much, he made haste with all the speed he could with his army, to come thither. But when he understood that Cato had slain himself, writers do report he said thus:

> "O Cato, I **envy** thy death, since thou hast envied mine honour."

Indeed, had Cato been contented Caesar should have saved his life, he had not so much impaired his own honour, as he had augmented Caesar's glory. And yet what Caesar would have done, men make it doubtful, saving that they conjecture well of Caesar's clemency.

Epilogue

Cato was forty-eight years old when he died. His son suffered no injury from Caesar; but it is said he grew idle and dissipated.

[*omission for content*]

But his earlier stains were entirely wiped off by the bravery of his death. For in the Battle of Philippi, where he fought for his country's liberty against Caesar and Antony, when the ranks were breaking, he, scorning to flee, or to escape unknown, called out to the enemy, showed himself to them in front, and encouraged those of his party who stayed; and at length fell, and left his enemies full of admiration of his valour.

Nor was Porcia, the daughter of Cato, inferior to the rest of her family, for sober living and greatness of spirit. She was married to Brutus, who killed Caesar; was acquainted with the conspiracy; and ended her life as became one of her birth and virtue. All which is related in the *Life of Brutus.*

Statilius, who said he would imitate Cato, was at that time hindered by the philosophers, when he would have put an end to his life. He afterwards followed Brutus, to whom he was very faithful and very serviceable, and died in the field of Philippi.

Narration and Discussion

"…all the people of Utica also came thither, and with one voice called Cato their benefactor and saviour, and said he only was a free man, and had an invincible mind." If they had done this before Cato's death, might he have changed his mind?

Later on, people wondered whether Caesar would have put Cato to death, or forgiven him. What do you think?

For older students: "Indeed, had Cato been contented Caesar should have saved his life, he had not so much impaired his own honour, as he had augmented Caesar's glory." What did Plutarch mean by this?

Examination Questions

Younger Students:

1. a) Tell what you know of Cato's childhood, both what he was like and the world around him.
   b) Plutarch said that Cato's attempt to make Caesar and Pompey be friends caused "the whole destruction of the empire of Rome." Can you explain why?

Older Students:

1. "All the troops desired him to be their leader; Scipio, likewise; and Varus gave way to it, and offered him the command; but he said he would not break those laws which he sought to defend ." Give some other examples of Cato's passion for. law and justice.

2. (High school) "Yet what most of all virtue and excellence fixed his affection was that steady and inflexible justice which is not to be wrought upon by favour or compassion." Explain and illustrate.

Bibliography

Plutarch's Lives of the Noble Greeks and Romans. Englished by Sir Thomas North. With an introduction by George Wyndham. Volume II. London: Dent, 1894. (Alcibiades, Coriolanus)

Plutarch's Lives of the Noble Greeks and Romans. Englished by Sir Thomas North. With an introduction by George Wyndham. Volume V. London: Dent, 1894. (Cato Utican)

Plutarch's Lives: The Dryden Plutarch. Revised by Arthur Hugh Clough, Volume I. London: J.M. Dent, 1910. (Alcibiades, Coriolanus)

Plutarch's Lives: The Dryden Plutarch. Revised by Arthur Hugh Clough, Volume III. London: J.M. Dent, 1910. (Cato the Younger)

About the Author

Anne E. White (www.annewrites.ca) has shared her knowledge of Charlotte Mason's methods through magazine columns, online writing, and conference workshops. She is an Advisory member of AmblesideOnline and the author of *Minds More Awake: The Vision of Charlotte Mason*, as well as other books in The Plutarch Project series.

Made in the USA
Las Vegas, NV
20 July 2023